MARK THESE MEN

Books by DR. J. SIDLOW BAXTER

AWAKE MY HEART
A devotional Bible study for every day in the year.

DOES GOD STILL GUIDE?
An answer to this important question in our time.

EXPLORE THE BOOK
A basic, progressive, interpretative course of Bible study, six volumes in one, from Genesis to Revelation.

GOD SO LOVED
An exposition of John 3:16, the best-known text in the Bible.

GOING DEEPER
A series of devotional studies in knowing, loving, and serving our Lord Jesus Christ.

HIS DEEPER WORK IN US
A further enquiry into New Testament teaching on the subject of Christian Holiness.

HIS PART AND OURS
Enriching exposition and devotional studies in the reciprocal union of Christ and His people.

MARK THESE MEN
Arresting studies of little understood aspects of Bible characters with special relevance for our times.

RETHINKING OUR PRIORITIES
A heart-to-heart talk with the church: its pastor and people.

STRATEGIC GRASP OF THE BIBLE
The marvelous design and structure of the Scriptures, with a discussion of the dispensational characteristics of biblical revelation.

STUDIES IN PROBLEM TEXTS
The problem texts of the Bible in patient and painstaking investigation.

CHRISTIAN HOLINESS: RESTUDIED AND RESTATED
Three works on the scriptural teaching on personal holiness, combined in one volume: *A New Call to Holiness, His Deeper Work in Us, Our High Calling*. These three are also available individually.

MARK THESE MEN

*Practical Studies in striking aspects
of certain Bible characters*

J. SIDLOW BAXTER

**ZONDERVAN
PUBLISHING HOUSE**
OF THE ZONDERVAN CORPORATION | GRAND RAPIDS, MICHIGAN 49506

Fifteenth printing 1978
ISBN 0-310-20671-5

Printed in the United States of America

FOREWORD

PERHAPS is it only fair, both to reader and writer, just to mention that the studies which make up this book were preached before they were printed. That accounts for their style of presentation. They were used in the course of my ministry at Charlotte Baptist Chapel, Edinburgh; and it is because of appreciations expressed that they are now sent out with the hope that perhaps in print they may have a usefulness to a wider circle. As will be noticed, the final study is considerably longer than the others. This is because it really combines three Sunday morning studies in one.

The biographical treasures of the Bible are exhaustless. Again and again we turn back to the figures which move before us in its pages, and find new relevances, new significances, new applications to our own times and to our own lives. Somehow, these Scripture characters seem to be invested with typological and representative qualities which live for all time. May the following unpretentious interpretations bring this home again with godly profit to the reader.

J. S. B.

This book, in its English edition, is dedicated with affectionate esteem to

ROBERT AITKEN, ESQ.

Beloved Elder at Charlotte Baptist Chapel, Edinburgh, with grateful remembrance of many kindnesses and loyal help in the ministry of the Gospel.

CONTENTS

THE MAN WHO DEFIED BAAL

SCRIPTURE SNAPSHOT

And it came to pass, when Ahab saw Elijah, that Ahab said unto him, Is it thou, thou troubler of Israel? And he answered, I have not troubled Israel, but thou, and thy father's house, in that ye have forsaken the commandments of the Lord, and thou hast followed the Baalim. Now therefore send, and gather to me all Israel unto mount Carmel, and the prophets of Baal four hundred and fifty, and the prophets of the Asherah four hundred, which eat at Jezebel's table.

So Ahab sent unto all the children of Israel, and gathered the prophets together unto mount Carmel. And Elijah came near unto all the people, and said, How long halt ye between two opinions? if the Lord be God, follow Him; but if Baal, then follow him. And the people answered him not a word. Then said Elijah unto the people, I, even I only, am left a prophet of the Lord; but Baal's prophets are four hundred and fifty men. Let them therefore give us two bullocks; and let them choose one bullock for themselves, and cut it in pieces, and lay it on the wood, and put no fire under: and I will dress the other bullock, and lay it on the wood, and put no fire under. And call ye on the name of your god, and I will call on the name of the Lord: and the God that answereth by fire, let him be God. And all the people answered, and said, It is well spoken ... ... And it came to pass at the time of the offering of the evening oblation, that Elijah the prophet came near, and said, O Lord, the God of Abraham, of Isaac, and of Israel, let it be known this day that Thou art God in Israel, and that I am Thy servant, and that I have done all these things at Thy word. Hear me, O Lord, hear me, that this people may know that Thou, Lord, art God, and that Thou hast turned their heart back again. Then the fire of the Lord fell, and consumed the burnt offering, and the wood, and the stones, and the dust, and licked up the water that was in the trench. And when all the people saw it, they fell on their faces: and they said, The Lord, He is God; the Lord, He is God.—1 Kings xviii. 17-39 (R.V.).

THE MAN WHO DEFIED BAAL

ELIJAH is one of the most remarkable figures in the history of Israel. His outstanding importance is seen both in the religious reformation which he wrought in his nation, and in the fact that the New Testament speaks of him more often than of any other Old Testament prophet. Moreover, it was Elijah who was chosen to appear with Moses at our Lord's transfiguration, to speak with Him there concerning His "exodus" which He should accomplish at Jerusalem. One able writer goes so far as to say that Elijah is the "grandest and most romantic character that Israel ever produced". Certainly, this prophet's giant proportions make him a kind of prophet-Hercules among men.

He suddenly appears on the scene as the crisis-prophet, with thunder on his brow and tempest in his voice. He disappears just as suddenly, being swept skyward in a chariot of fire. Between his first appearing and his final disappearing lies a succession of amazing miracles. The very style of the narrative is marked by a vividness and beauty which stamp this prophet of fire on the imagination; and in later times he has come to us with fresh dramatic beauty in the glorious music of Mendelssohn's oratorio.

We shall here speak of three things about him—his character, his ministry, his significance.

HIS CHARACTER

The grandeur of Elijah's character is recognised by us all. Even those critics of the Bible who have disputed Elijah's miracles have allowed the greatness of his character. He seems to have been somewhat remarkable even *physically*. He was not a man of the city, but of the open country. Indeed, he seems to have been a veritable bedouin, loving the haunts of the hills and valleys, and roaming the broad, unsettled pasturages of Bashan. His rugged and austere appearance would be such as at once to attract the eye of the softer-clad townsman. When we read of Elijah's confronting Ahab, and announcing the coming drought, we must picture the shaggy-bearded, long-haired, weather-tanned sheik, or the gaunt, piercing-eyed dervish, clad with a rough sheep-skin, striding into the king's presence, and lifting up a sinewy arm to heaven as he denounces the weak-willed king in tones sounding like awesome echoes from the mountains.

But Elijah is no less striking in his *moral* character. Three qualities are especially conspicuous—courage, faith and zeal. See his *courage*. Here is the man who bearded the beast in its very lair, the man who strode into the king's audience-chamber and denounced the king to his face, in the name of Jehovah. Here is the Martin Luther of old-time Israel, who, single-handed, challenged the whole priesthood of the State religion, and all the people of the realm, to the decisive test on Mount Carmel. And if, in a moment of overwroughtness, he fled at Jezebel's threat, let us be quick to perceive that he did not flee because he feared Jezebel more than the treacherous Ahab or the powerful priests of Baal, but because, for the moment, he lost heart through a sudden and sickening set-back to the great religious reformation which he was bringing about. The fire of Jehovah had just fallen on Carmel. King and people together had witnessed it, and had fallen prostrate, exclaiming, "Jehovah, He is the God! Jehovah, He is the God!" And now, just as Elijah thinks the demonstration has been conclusive and that the whole nation will forthwith return to Jehovah, there comes this blood-thirsty threat from the highest power in the land. Instead of having become convinced by truth, the queen had become filled with the fury of a demon. For the moment, the discouraged champion recoils. Quickly making away from the crowds, he hastes to a lonely place and sinks down exhausted under a Juniper bush. That Juniper bush incident certainly shows the prophet's humanness; but that very touch of humanness makes his otherwise consistent boldness the more commendable and striking.

See also Elijah's *faith*. It was his faith which underlay his courage. A faith like Elijah's gives courage like a lion's. What faith it required to go before Ahab and say: "There shall not be dew nor rain these years, but according to my word"! Dew and rain may be withheld, through ordinary natural causes, for days, or even weeks, or in rare cases, for some months; but for dew and rain to be suspended for years, as Elijah declared they would be, involved supernatural intervention. Such intervention Elijah had prayed for; and he believed that God would certainly answer, for the sake of vindicating the truth in Israel. This dauntless faith shines out through all the record.

Then see Elijah's *zeal*. How truly did he express the over-mastering passion of his being when, at the mouth of the cave on Horeb, he said, "I have been very jealous for the Lord God of hosts"! How much this sun-bronzed, untutored child of the desert can teach us of jealousy for the Divine honour, of burning indignation at religious compromise and of passionate loyalty to the word of God! See him away yonder, among the highlands of Gilead, with troubled look and appealing prayer to God, as snatches of news, followed by more definite accounts, make known to him the dark doings in Israel—Jezebel's destruction of Jehovah's altars and priests, the installation of her strange Tyrian gods with their hideous forms of worship, the treacherous behaviour of Ahab, and the shameful apostasy of the people at large. Elijah can forbear no longer. He must go! The honour of Jehovah is at stake! And so begins Elijah's public ministry. Well has he been called the prophet of fire. There is a burning intensity about his godliness. Would that some of the liquid fire that ran in this man's veins might course through our own as we see the unholy religious tolerations of our own day and generation.

HIS MINISTRY

And now think briefly of Elijah's *ministry*. Old Dr. Kitto remarks: "There are two sorts of prophets; prophets of deeds, and prophets of words. Of the latter the greatest is doubtless Isaiah: of the former there has not been among men a greater than Elijah." This, then, is the first thing about Elijah's ministry

—he was a prophet of *deeds*. So far as we know, he wrote nothing; and this does not surprise us; for such devout impetuosity and tempestuousness as Elijah's seldom go with patient penmanship. Many of the most passionate and energetic reformers have been altogether ungifted as writers. They were men of action rather than diction. They were dynamic rather than academic. They flung themselves with passionate abandon into the effort of prevailing upon the men of their own day. They may not have perpetuated their names in books which have been handed on to succeeding generations; but they live on, none the less, in the abiding results of the exploits which they wrought for the betterment of their fellows. Such an one was Elijah. He was emphatically a prophet to his own day. He was the man of prompt action, of strong measures and explosive deeds. There is always a need for such men. Perhaps they are specially needed in our own day.

But again, Elijah's ministry was one of *miracles*. At every turn of the story miracles meet us; and because of this, many recent scholars have summarily discarded this section of Scripture as being largely mythical. Yet the narrative is so sober and circumstantial that had it not been for this element in it, the most destructive critic would never have questioned its veracity. In other words, the narrative is doubted simply *because* it records miracles. But these miracles are no stumbling-block to those who are unprejudiced. Nay, we rather see in them a *proof* of veracity; for if ever there was a time in Israel's history when miracles were *needed* it was in Ahab and Jezebel's time. Unprecedented corruption loudly called for such a drastic mission as Elijah's—a mission armed with such signs and wonders as should be unmistakable credentials of its divine authority.

Once again, Elijah's ministry was one of *reformation*. He did not originate anything new. He was a protestant against the religious apostasy and resultant degradation of his nation; and he called men back to the good old ways which Israel's covenant-keeping God had marked out for them through Moses. There is need to-day for such outright, honest protestantism. Let us not refrain simply for comfort's sake from protesting against those things which dishonour our Saviour's name and cause. Some people scorn such protesting on the ground that protesting is merely a negative procedure. But there is a place for the negative as well as the positive. There is a place for pulling down as well as for building up. There is a place for slum-clearance as well as for new-villa building. There is a place for attacking error as well as for proclaiming truth. We need Elijahs to-day just as much as we need Isaiahs. May we not be afraid to follow Elijah's lead!

HIS SIGNIFICANCE

We come now to the heart of our subject. What is Elijah's permanent significance? How do the character and ministry of this extraordinary man speak to the people of God to-day? Well, first of all, Elijah demonstrates the truth that *God always has a man to match the hour*. The Almighty never yet failed to provide the right man for any time of serious emergency. The man required for the vital task or for the critical juncture is infallibly singled out and prepared for his work. Where the demands of the situation are such that ordinary gifts and attainments will not suffice, the man is appointed for his work from childhood or even before his birth; so that just when the zero hour comes, and the gathered forces of evil seem about to riot in tragic victory, God's prepared champion stands forth and strikes the mighty blow that brings victory out of threatened destruction.

See the state of things in Elijah's day. It could scarcely have been worse. After the reigns of Saul and David and Solomon, ten of the Hebrew tribes had revolted and constituted themselves a separate kingdom. Their first king had been that wicked man, Jeroboam, whose distinguishing epitaph is: "Jeroboam, the son of Nebat, which made Israel to sin." This is the Jeroboam who put a golden calf at Dan in the north and another at Bethel in the south, as representations of the invisible Jehovah, for the people to worship. After Jeroboam's death, about forty years had passed when *Ahab* came to the throne. During that intervening forty years, there had been a continued moral and religious deterioration. No less than six kings had reigned, and all had been evil. Things were dark enough when Ahab began to reign, but he quickly made them a hundred times worse. It is written of him:

"He did evil above all that were before him." "There was none like unto Ahab, which did sell himself to work wickedness in the sight of the Lord, whom Jezebel his wife stirred up. And he did very abominably in following idols according to all things as did the Amorites whom the Lord cast out before the children of Israel." "Ahab did more to provoke the Lord God of Israel to anger than all the kings of Israel that were before him." Jezebel, his heathen wife, was a handsome, shrewd and intriguing woman who worked her will through the evil-hearted but weak-willed Ahab with sinister skill. She was the daughter of Ethbaal, king of the Zidonians, and caused Ahab to worship her abominable Baalim. Then under the royal lead, a grimly determined effort was made to stamp out the religion of Jehovah from Israel once for all. The altars of Jehovah were cast down, and the prophets were murdered. In their place groves to false gods were erected, hundreds of heathen priests took possession and were sustained from the revenues of the royal purse. Licentious modes of worship were introduced. Temples to Baalim were built at Jezreel and Samaria. It was the darkest hour in the spiritual history of Israel. The prevalence of idolatry appeared to be complete. It seemed as though the crushed worship of Jehovah could never regain its lost prestige and power. The elect nation which had been chosen to be the repository of Divine truth seemed to have lapsed into an incurable heathenism and abominableness.

Yet just at this zero hour God's champion arises. The times are calling for an Elijah; and an Elijah appears! As Bishop Hall says, "The greatest prophet is reserved for the worst age. Israel never had such an impious king as Ahab, nor such a miraculous prophet as Elijah."

The same thing is seen again and again in history. When the light of evangelical truth seems on the point of being quite extinguished from Christendom, and Popery smothers Europe's millions beneath its evil cloak, God has His Martin Luthers and John Calvins to call back the continent to the faith once for all delivered to the saints. When politics and religion and morals become so degraded in Britain that the very vitals of the nation are jeopardised, God has His John Wycliffes and William Tyndales and George Whitefields and John Wesleys. And in these days of the twentieth century, when the enemy has come in like a flood, we shall find again that the Spirit of the Lord will lift up a standard against him. God will match the hour with a modern Elijah. No doubt in Elijah's dark day there were many secret prayers ascending to God for some gracious intervention; and God did not fail to answer. When Satan turns out prodigies of evil such as Ahab and Jezebel and Hitler and Mussolini, God can raise up spiritual giants like Elijah who shall put them down. Let us fervently pray God to do this in our own day!

Another thing which Elijah demonstrates to us is that *when wickedness develops into extraordinary proportions God meets it with extraordinary measures.* The Phœnician gods which Jezebel and Ahab had taught Israel to worship were largely emblems of the material elements which produce dew and rain—Baal, Ashtoreth, and Ashere. Therefore Israel's *true* God will now show His superiority over all the material elements and powers of nature which the Phœnicians worshipped, by suspending the rain and dew for three years and six months! Over against the superstitions and fake miracles of the false religion, Jehovah will now intervene with a special succession of *real* miracles which will vindicate the true faith of Israel against all impostures. *This* is why the ministry of Elijah is one of miracles. God is meeting an extraordinary situation by extraordinary measures.

Now I believe that in the later days of this present age, when undoubtedly an extraordinary situation has begun to develop, we may expect God once again to meet the challenge by extraordinary measures. Those of the Lord's people in Britain who have not bowed the knee to Baal nor kissed his image should be praying daily and hourly to God to meet the unprecedented situation by some corresponding measure. If we cannot withdraw for secret prayer as often as we would, let us be asking God in between our daily tasks. The apostle James tells us that it was prayer which brought God's startling intervention in Elijah's day. He says: "Elias was a man subject to like passions as we are, and he prayed that it might not rain: and it rained not on the earth by the space of three years and six months." So the drought was an answer to prayer! "Oh," exclaims someone, "how dreadful of Elijah to pray for such a calamity! Think of all the people who would

suffer, especially the women and children!" Yes, but far worse
than Elijah's praying for the drought was the fact that such a
prayer was *needed*. Elijah was a man who had enough sound-
ness of judgment to know that physical suffering is a far smaller
calamity than ungodliness and moral failure. Even a long
drought, despite the physical suffering it might inflict, would be
a kindness if it brought the people back to God, and saved their
souls, and purified their morals. Far better that drought be sent
to scourge the people back to the true God than that they should
degrade themselves more and more amid the licentious orgies of
Baal and Astarte! There are many people who never do any
decisive good because they cannot be severe. Such people would
have pleaded with Elijah not to pray for the drought; and they
would have recoiled with horror that Elijah should think of slaying the several hundred prophets of Baal. "Oh," they would have
argued, "but some of the priests are such nice fellows; they are
real gentlemen, and so sympathetic in their manner." Such are
the people who to-day, with sickly kindness, will tolerate teachers
of error in our pulpits because they are such smooth-mannered
and amiable gentlemen. They would rather allow error to be
preached and souls to be deceived than hurt the preacher's feelings. Let Baal be worshipped rather than drought come! Let
the cancer kill its victim rather than the cruel surgeon use the
knife! Let the disease run its course rather than enforce the bitter
medicine! The best thing that could happen to some so-called
Christian ministers of to-day is that they should be denounced in
God's name by their hearers. To be kind and tolerant to them is
to be cruel to their long-suffering congregations. Why should they
be allowed to exploit the Christian pulpit and live on the revenues
of the Church for the preaching of modern thought instead of
Divine truth? Severe dealing is required. Maybe if they were
turned out of the Church many of those who now *stay* out would
turn in again to hear what the word of the Lord is!

But to re-emphasize what we were saying, may we not expect
that in these abnormal days God will meet the situation by some
super-normal means? I think we may. Let us keep laying hold
upon God for some present-day display of the old-time power of
the Gospel such as shall confound the Lord's enemies, and light

the fires of evangelical revival throughout our land! Some of the Lord's people are sighing: "Oh it's no use praying for revival to-day. No big revival is prophesied in Scripture for the end of the present age. Things are just to go from bad to worse until the Lord's second coming." What a paralysing idea this is! Quite apart from anything else it is enough to cut the nerve of prayer and faith. Yet what a foolish misconception it is! Where in prophecy do we find any mention of the Tyndale revival, the Puritan revival, the Wesleyan revival? Yet these, and other glorious visitations from heaven came, and are gratefully chronicled in the annals of our nation. What is more, we would ask: Where is there any place in Scripture which says that there *cannot* or *will not* be another such revival in our own day? Let us cry mightily that our God may do a new thing for us in these days; that He may match His method to the need of the hour, and cause the praises of Jesus once again, even in *our* day, to resound over our hills and valleys.

There are many other ways in which Elijah is significant for us to-day; but we will mention just one more. *Elijah is to come to this earth again!* Strikingly enough, we are told this in the very last words with which the Old Testament closes:

"Behold, I will send you Elijah the prophet before the coming of the great and dreadful day of the Lord; and he shall turn the heart of the fathers to the children, and the heart of the children to their parents, lest I come and smite the earth with a curse" (Mal. iv. 5–6).

The "great and dreadful day of the Lord" has yet to come, as the New Testament clearly teaches us. It is that dread event which will wind up the present dispensation. It will coincide with Armageddon, when the winepress of God's wrath will be trodden in Divine fury against the earth's wicked-doers. The second coming of the Lord Jesus Christ as King and Judge is rapidly nearing as this age rushes on with gathering momentum to its terrific culmination: but before the long pent-up "wrath of God" breaks loose against the "man of sin" and his vile armies, Elijah is to come and warn men that "the day of the Lord" is at hand.

Turn to the eleventh chapter of the Book of Revelation. This awesome chapter carries us on to the last three and a half years of the present age. See what it says:

> "And I will give power unto My two witnesses, and they shall prophesy a thousand two hundred and threescore days, clothed in sackcloth. And if any man will hurt them, fire proceedeth out of their mouth, and devoureth their enemies; and if any man will hurt them he must in this manner be killed."

And who are these two prophet-witnesses? Well, let us read on, and see how the description of their ministry identifies them.

> "These have power to shut heaven, that it rain not in the days of their prophecy; and have power over waters to turn them to blood, and to smite the earth with all plagues as often as they will."

The shutting of heaven and causing of drought immediately suggests Elijah, while the turning of water to blood and the inflicting of plagues, immediately suggests Moses.

Here, then, right at the end of this age, are Moses and Elijah back again!—for unless we spiritualise the whole of this Book of Revelation and thereby land ourselves in a quagmire of hopeless difficulties, we cannot but see, from the description and details in this eleventh chapter, that two real persons are here intended, just as the other actors in the chapter are meant to be taken as real persons.

Now this reappearance of Moses and Elijah, in Revelation xi, completes a significant chain of Scripture references. First, in the account of our Lord's transfiguration we are told that there appeared *"two men* which were Moses and Elias," and that they spoke with Him about "His decease (literally His *'Exodus')* which He should accomplish at Jerusalem." Thus, at the Lord's *transfiguration,* these two men, Moses and Elijah, bear witness to the meaning of His *crucifixion.* Next, we are told that on the morning of our Saviour's resurrection *"two men"* suddenly stood by, "in shining garments." Thus these "two men" bear witness to the *resurrection*.

Again, at the Lord's *ascension*, "While they (the disciples) looked steadfastly toward heaven as He went up, behold *two men* stood by them in white apparel, which also said: Ye men of Galilee, why stand ye gazing up into heaven? This same Jesus, which is taken up from you into heaven, shall so come in like manner as ye have seen Him go into heaven." Thus, these two men now bear witness at our Lord's *ascension*, and point on to His *second coming*.

Finally, in this eleventh chapter of Revelation, we see them back again; but this time they have taken off their "white apparel" and "shining garments," and are "clothed in sackcloth"; for they have come to give final warning against sin, and final warning of "the wrath to come"!

There are those who scorn the idea that Elijah will thus come again, just as they deny a literal second coming of the Lord Jesus. They hold that the prophecies of Isaiah and Malachi concerning the coming of Elijah were fulfilled in John the Baptist, speaking of whom our Lord said: "Elias is come already." There certainly is a sense in which John the Baptist was Elijah; for he came "in the spirit and power of Elias" (Luke i. 17), as the Lord's fore-runner, according to the prophecies of Isaiah and Malachi. But John was not Elijah *personally*. He was simply an interim and provisional fulfilment of the Elijah prophecies, as a careful examination of our Lord's words about him clearly shows. When the disciples asked: "Why then say the scribes that Elias must first come?" our Lord significantly employed first the future tense and then the past tense in His reply. "Elias *is indeed coming first*," He says, "and he *shall restore* all things." (These words, which clearly look to the future, would be very strange if they referred to John the Baptist, for John was now already dead!) Then the Lord continues: "But I say unto you that Elias is come already, and they knew him not, but have done unto him whatsover they listed." (*These* words *do* refer to John the Baptist, as the disciples clearly understood—Matthew xvii. 10–13.) Indeed, while recognising in John a figurative and partial fulfilment of the Elijah prophecies, our Lord actually speaks of him as having now become in turn an adumbration of the real and personal Elijah who is *still to come*; for He says (translating His words in Matthew xi. 14 literally): "This (John) is Elias, *who is about to come*." John himself, in answer to the question: "Art thou Elias?" said: "I am not" (John i. 21). Yet although self-confessedly he was not Elijah *personally*, John himself just as clearly claimed to be the promised Elijah-like forerunner; for he said: "I am the voice of one crying in the wilderness; make straight the way of the Lord, as said the prophet Esaias," and in these words he at once identified himself with Isaiah xl. Thus, in a figurative sense, Elijah came in John the Baptist; but in the literal and personal sense, he is still to come at the end of the present age, as shown in Revelation xi. Just as the first coming of the Lord Jesus only partly fills the Messianic prophecies of the Old Testament, and requires His second coming at the end of the present age; so the coming of John the Baptist at our Lord's first advent only provisionally fills the Elijah prophecies, and requires the literal return of Elijah at the end of the present age, before the coming of "the great and dreadful day of the Lord."

Elijah himself then, is really to come again. He witnesses in connection with the transfiguration, the crucifixion, the resurrection, the ascension, the second coming, and "the wrath to come"! Truly he is a significant figure. He tells us that God always has His man for the hour, that God always meets the extraordinary situation by some corresponding measure, that God never leaves Himself without witnesses, and that God has prepared, in sovereign wisdom, against all contingencies of the future. Yes, Elijah is to come back—and not only as the announcer of wrath, but as the precursor of the King of Kings, David's Son and Lord, even His royal majesty King Jesus. Well may our daily prayer be "Even so, Lord Jesus, come quickly"!

THE MAN WHO PLAYED THE FOOL

SCRIPTURE SNAPSHOT

Then Saul arose, and went down to the wilderness of Ziph, having three thousand chosen men of Israel with him, to seek David (i.e., to slay him) . . .

And David and Abishai came by night; and, behold, Saul lay sleeping within the place of the waggons, with his spear stuck in the ground at his head: and Abner and the people lay round about him. Then said Abishai to David: God hath delivered up thine enemy into thine hand this day; now therefore let me smite him. And David said to Abishai: Destroy him not; for who can put forth his hand against the Lord's anointed, and be guiltless? . . . But now take, I pray thee, the spear that is at his head, and the cruse of water, and let us go. . . .

Then David went over to the other side, and stood on the top of the mountain afar off . . . and David cried to the people: Answerest thou not Abner? . . . Wherefore, then, has thou not kept watch over thy lord, the king? . . . And now see where the king's spear is, and the cruse of water that was at his head. And Saul knew David's voice, and said: Is this thy voice, my son, David? . . . I have sinned; return, my son David; for I will no more do thee harm, because my life was precious in thine eyes this day. Behold, I have played the fool and have erred exceedingly.—

I Samuel xxvi. 2–21 (R.V.).

THE MAN WHO PLAYED THE FOOL

"Then said Saul . . . I have played the fool."
—1 Samuel xxvi. 21.

SAUL, the first king of Israel, is one of the most striking and tragic figures in the Old Testament. If we are at all sensitive as to the supreme values and vital issues of human life, the story of this man is bound to challenge us. We might profitably pick out this or that aspect of his character for separate consideration, but it is more important to see such a man in his totality, and to get the full impact of his significance. In some ways he is very big, and in others very little. In some ways he is commandingly handsome, and in others decidedly ugly. All in one he is a giant and a dwarf, a hero and a renegade, a king and a slave, a prophet and a reprobate, a man God-anointed, and a man Satan-possessed. He began so promisingly, yet deteriorated so dismally, and ended so ignominiously as to make the downgrade process which ruined him monumental for ever afterward to all who will read, mark, and learn.

Look comprehensively, then, at this man, and you will find yourself marvelling at three notable features or phases in his career: (1) his early promise; (2) his later failure; (3) his final ruin.

HIS EARLY PROMISE

Never did a young man show fairer promise or kindlier possibilities; and never did such a young man find more illustrious opportunities greeting him at the outset of his adult years. All this we find in 1 Samuel ix to xii.

To begin with, he was distinguished by a *striking physical superiority*. Chapter ix. 2 describes him as "a choice young man, and a goodly: there was not among the children of Israel a goodlier person than he: from his shoulders and upward he was higher than any of the people." Again, in Chapter x. 24, we read, "There is none like him among all the people." We mention this distinguishment of stature first, not because this was first in importance, but because it is the first thing to which the Scripture record calls attention. The physical is the less important part of man. Isaac Watts well says:

> I must be measured by my soul,
> The mind's the standard of the man.

Yet what an advantage is a fine physique! No lean-fleshed man of diminutive proportions will pretend that he does not wish he had the congenial benefits of health and height and handsomeness. Well, young Saul had these to the degree of striking superiority. He was the most handsomely proportioned young man in the land. And by this he had the initial advantage of being immediately prepossessing.

Second; young Saul revealed certain *highly commendable qualities of disposition*. The stateliness of his outward frame did not belie his inward stature. We note his *modesty*. When Samuel told him of the honour coming to him, he replied that he came of the least family in the smallest of the tribes, and counted himself unworthy of such honour (ix. 21). On the day of his public presentation he "hid himself among the stuff" (x. 22). We note also his *discreetness*. There was a despicable little minority who, even amid the general acclamation at Saul's investiture, sneered: "How shall this man save us?" The record says they were "the sons of Belial," that they "despised" Saul, and "brought him no presents" (x. 27). Oh, those "sons of Belial"! They are an evil seed which ever persists. There are human serpents who will slime any man's Eden, and envenom people against the best of public men. What did Saul do? One word from him in that electric hour, and the "sons of Belial" would have been assassinated to a man. Yet we read simply this: "But Saul held his peace." Still further, we note in young Saul *a very generous spirit*. In the flush of the young king's speedy victory against Israel's foes, the people as a whole clamour for the death of those who have spoken against their hero. Mark the magnanimity of Saul's reply—"There shall not a man be put to death this day; for to-day the Lord hath wrought salvation in Israel" (xi. 13). And there were other fine qualities in him too—his considerateness of others (ix. 5), his dash and courage (xi. 6, 11), his capacity for strong love, as shown towards both David and Jonathan (xvi. 21), his energetic antagonism to such evils as spiritism (xxviii. 3), and his quite evident moral purity in social relationships.

Third; we note *the special equipment which God gave to him,* when calling him to become Israel's king. We well realize, of course, that young Saul's first equipment was himself. Whenever God calls a man to some high vocation, he not only gives special equipments, he calls the one who by his very nature is the man for the work. This was true of Saul. He was kingly in himself. He had the right natural capacities and capabilities to begin with. But now to these were superadded certain remarkable equipments of a supernatural kind. First, he was given the inspired word of Samuel, "God is with thee" (x. 7). Then we read that "God gave him another heart" so that he became "another man" (x. 6, 9). Then again, we are told that "the Spirit of God came upon him, and he prophesied" (x. 10). These expressions cannot mean less than that Saul became inwardly renewed, and was under the special guidance of the Holy Spirit. Nor is this all. He was surrounded by a *"band* of men whose hearts God had touched" (x. 26); and the Hebrew word translated as a "band of men" really means the *host,* the men mighty in valour. Still further, he had that trusty counsellor and God-inspired prophet, Samuel, at his hand. And to crown all this, God signalized the commencement of his reign by granting a spectacular military victory which placed the new king high in the confidence of the people (xi. 12).

These, then, were some of the favourable factors which gilded young Saul's debut with such fair promise. Extraordinarily rich in natural endowments, and specially equipped by supernatural conferments, what shining heights looked like being scaled! Many a man has had outstanding opportunity but has lacked ability; and many another man has had outstanding ability but has lacked opportunity. Here, however, in the case of handsome young Saul, transcendent opportunity and transcendent ability matched each other. It was an opportunity in a million, coming to a man in a million. Certainly there were some difficulties implicit in the situation at the time; but that was simply because the opportunity was on earth and not in heaven! There never yet was an open "door of opportunity" without there being at least a few "adversaries" blocking the way to it. So far as Saul was concerned, all such discouragements were dwarfed by the bigness of his advantages and reassurances. He was called to kingship; and he was constitutionally kingly. He was called to *theocratic* kingship; and he was supernaturally equipped thereto. What scope for glorious co-operation with God! What opportunity to bless men! He was called to rule and shepherd the most wonderful nation in history. The possibilities were immense. And the gifted young champion began wonderfully well. He betrayed none of the symptoms of vainglory which others, far less gifted than himself, have revealed when abruptly elevated. His advent to the throne was indeed a daybreak of fair promise.

HIS LATER DECLINE

Alas, Saul's early promise is a quickly fading flower, a morning sky soon overcast with sullen clouds. How soon does the gold "become dim" and the fine gold as an "earthen pitcher"! Defection, declension, degeneration, disaster—that is the dismal downgrade which now develops, until our giant-hero drops as a haggard suicide into ignominious death. Let us briefly inspect the downgrade process as it reveals itself outwardly, and then see what lay behind it inwardly.

Saul's first grave defection occurred early. See chapter xiii. It was an act of *irreverent presumption*. God intended that Saul should free Israel from the Philistines (ix. 16). Saul gathered a small but picked army, and purposely offended the Philistines by smiting one of their garrisons in Israel. This brought the might of Philistia against him, compared with which his own quickly scared and dwindling handful looked contemptible. Saul was expressly bidden to wait seven days in Gilgal, for Samuel.

It was a necessary test. Saul failed badly. The seventh day wore
on, and Samuel did not seem to be coming. Saul, in wilful impatience, violated the priest's prerogative, and foolishly presumed to offer up with his own hand the pre-arranged sacrifices
to the Lord.

We can allow for Saul's predicament. The Philistines, presumably, might attack at any moment, and Saul's position in
the plain was one of acute risk. Yet he knew that obedience to
the voice of God through the prophet was a basic condition of
his theocratic kingship. His impatience really amounted to dis-
trust of Jehovah. His presumptuous offering was not really
because of concern to propitiate God, but to impress the people
(xiii. 8). He would be a prudent general rather than an obedient
servant of God. He ignored the fact that although he was the
earthly king of Israel he was in turn the servant of Israel's
heavenly King, Whom it was his duty to obey. "Saul, thou
hast done foolishly," says Samuel. "Thou has not kept the commandment of Jehovah." Saul knew it: yet he made no confession either of wrong or regret.

Saul's *second* default follows quickly on the first. See chapter xiv. It is an act of *rash wilfulness*. By a supernatural intervention God spares Israel a debacle at the hands of the Philistines. Jonathan, Saul's son, is His instrument. Confusion spreads
among the enemy. They mistakenly slay each other. Israel's
watchmen report what they see. Saul calls Ahijah the priest to
ask of the Lord concerning this, but with stupid impatience cuts
short the enquiry and rushes off with his forces without guidance
(xiv. 18–20, R.V.). He also rashly imposes a curse of death on
any man who should eat food that day (24), with the result that
his men were too weak to exploit the God-given victory to the
full (30), and with the further result that his hunger-stricken
helpers sinned by eating flesh with the blood (32), and with the
further grave outcome that Jonathan came under the death sen-
tence through ignorance of the curse, and would have been slain
if not rescued by the people (27, 45). "Saul, thou hast done
foolishly!"

But now, in chapter xv, comes still worse default, a blend
of *disobedience and deceit*. Saul is told to destroy utterly the

vile Amalekites; but he spares the king and the best live-stock. Then he equivocates to Samuel. He slips blame for the booty on to the people. He even pretends the booty is for sacrifice to Jehovah. The episode marks a distinct breakdown in his character. Samuel's rebuke begins, "When thou was little in thine own sight . . ." Humility had now been ousted by arrogance. Samuel sees right through the sham to the real. He calls the default "rebellion" and "stubbornness." "Wherefore didst thou not obey?" "Thou hast rejected the word of Jehovah."

From this point Saul's decline is steep. "The Spirit of the Lord departed from Saul" (xvi. 14). Nor is that all: an "evil spirit" troubled him (14 etc.). He goes rapidly from bad to worse. He gives way to a petty jealousy of young David until it becomes a fiendish malice. Thrice he tries to kill him. Then he hunts him like "a partridge on the mountains," for months on end. He is now giving way to the basest in himself. Twice David spares Saul's life. Twice Saul promises to desist. He knew that in hunting David's blood he was actually fighting God; for he admitted, "I know well that thou shalt surely be king" (xxiv. 20); yet even after that, he resumed his dastardly pursuit.

Mark this man. This big-souled giant is shrivelling into a shrimp. This kingly hero is becoming a toad beneath the heel of his own sadistic moods and passions. When he was little in his own eyes he was really big; but the bigger he has grown in his own eyes, the less he has become. When he was simple and godly he was truly great; but when he opened the door to disobedience and presumption and pride and pretence and jealousy and hatred, he sold himself to the devil and disaster. Every now and then his better self broke through and spoke again, but its protests became weaker and weaker as sin more and more got the mastery. He has engraved his own pathetic epitaph for us in the words of our text—"*I have played the fool.*"

But what was it that lay *behind* this man's fearful self-frustration? We may answer in a word: it was *self-will*. Saul's two besetting sins were presumption and disobedience to God; and behind both these was impulsive, unsubdued self-will. His self-frustration was self-assertion instead of self-submission. We may trace the four progressive stages of this ruinous self-ism in Saul:

first self-sensitiveness, then self-assertiveness, then self-centredness, increasingly issuing in self-destructiveness.

HIS FINAL FAILURE

The last tragic act in the mournful drama of this man Saul is depicted in chapters xxviii to xxxi. His downgrade course at length brings him to the witch of Endor, as an embittered, desolate-hearted fugitive from doom. This giant wreck of a man who once enjoyed direct counsel from heaven now traffics with the underworld! To choose "self" in preference to God is, in its ultimate meaning and outcome, to choose the devil. We need not dilate on Saul's midnight consultation with the witch, nor on his battlefield suicide the next day. There is no need to pick on details. It is enough simply to know the stark fact, the final plunge—witchcraft and suicide. Saul is no more. He lies a corpse, with lovely Jonathan. How are the mighty fallen! How is this son of the morning brought to shame! Yes, Saul!—Saul of early promise but of rapid decline and final ruin, you have "played the fool."

And now, with the final failure of this man before us, we do well to ask what are the main lessons which his story utters to us. Some of these lessons are so obvious that they scarcely need pointing out; but they are so urgent and vital that they call for earnest re-emphasis. Two, at least, of the lessons which come to us through this man's life are fundamental; the others are incidental.

First, then, king Saul preaches to us that *the one vital condition for the true fulfilment of life is obedience to the will of God;* and by "obedience" here we mean loyalty to the word and will of God both in inward motive and in outward action. The hidden root from which those evil shoots grew which eventually strangled the best in Saul was self-will. The fundamental fault was that he had never really surrendered his will to God. We ought to mark well the fact that Saul was called to a *theocratic* kingship —because we too are called to the same. Every human personality is meant to be a kind of theocracy. Saul was never meant to have kingship in the sense of absolute power. It was never intended that the last word should be with *him*. He was not merely "appointed" by *men*, to exert his own will over his fellows; he was "anointed" of *God* to be the executor of a will higher than his own. He was the human and visible vice-regent of Israel's divine and invisible King, Jehovah. He could only rightly rule the subjects under him insofar as he obeyed the will of the supreme King above him.

So is it with ourselves. Every human personality, we repeat, is meant to be a theocracy. You and I are not the independent proprietors of our own being and existence. We are God's property. All that we have, God gave us. All that we are, that is good, God made us. We are strips of territory which lie within His proper domain. God has made us kings. He has made us kings over our own personalities, with their gifts and powers and capacities and possibilities; but our kingship is meant to be theocratic, not an independent, self-determined monarchy. We are meant to reign and rule for *God,* so that our lives and personalities may fulfil His will, and accomplish His purpose, and be a blessing to other human beings, and a praise to God Himself. When we obstinately reign—or think we are reigning—independently of God, our real kingship breaks down, we miss the real meaning and purpose of life, and, whether we realize it soon or late, we "play the fool."

Now with most, if not all of us, this is the very centre-point of our controversy with God. We are prepared to do almost anything rather than hand over our own will to God. Look at Saul again: he was willing to be quite religious, willing for service, willing even for "sacrifice"—the costliest and most religious of all acts, but he stopped short at the one vital point. It was this which drew from Samuel's lips those memorable words, "TO OBEY IS BETTER THAN (EVEN) SACRIFICE." God help us to learn this fundamental lesson!

But further, and closely akin to what we have just said, Saul illustrates to us that *to let "self" get the upper hand in our life is to miss the best and court the worst.* It is to end by saying, "I have played the fool." By "self" here we do not simply mean "selfish." We do not get the impression that Saul himself was selfish by nature: he seems to have been rather the other way.

Yet he allowed himself to become self-conscious, then self-pre-ferring, then self-asserting, until he became more and more self-centred and self-destroying. Oh, this subtle, insidious "self," this wretched, hereditary legacy from Adam! How it loves to be taken notice of! How it pretends! How it equivocates! How it deceives! And how it ruins us when it gets the upper hand! The Philistines were not Saul's most dangerous enemies. His worst foe was himself.

So is it indeed with ourselves. Our biggest enemies are not our "circumstances"—as we usually try to persuade ourselves and others. Our deadliest peril is this "fifth-columnist" inside our own skin. Only let this Hitler get his jack-boot on our necks, and he will tread us down until all that is really worthy is crushed out of us. Every man who lets self fill his vision till it blinds his inward eye to what is true and divine is playing the fool. All of us who are living for self in preference to the will of God are playing the fool. The downgrade process in our life may not be as observable outwardly as it was in the career of Saul, simply because we do not occupy as conspicuous and peculiar a posi-tion as he did; yet we are just as really playing the fool. Our end on earth may not be as spectacular and outwardly tragic as Saul's was, yet our ultimate ruin is just as certain, and our remorse will be equally useless.

There are thousands of souls even now in Hades, lifting up their eyes in torments because in their days on earth they played the fool. When they inhabited bodies, and lived on earth, they were not drunkards or blasphemers or grossly licentious persons. Many of them were complimented on their respectability. But as to the things which really matter—the word of God, the will of God, the Christ of God, the Spirit of God, the Gospel of God, the ultimate issues of life, heaven, hell, eternity—as to these things they played the fool. They preferred self-will to God's will; they lived for themselves; they remained complacently and will-ingly ignorant concerning the first obligations of life, and politely ignored God. They missed the real meaning and purpose of life; they lived and died alienated from God; and now, in Hades, as they await the final judgment-day before the Great White Throne. their unavailing confession is, "I have played the fool."

But let us not forget this, either: it is not only in the Beyond that this confession is wrung from souls. If we choose the way of self-will in preference to the will of God, there is no knowing to what depths of sin and shame and suffering and sorrow it may reduce us, even in this present brief life. The simply awful fact is that *we are not safe* until we have learned to say with utter earnestness,

> Take my will, and make it Thine,
> It shall be no longer mine.
> Take my heart, it is Thine own,
> It shall be Thy royal throne.

But glance back yet again at this man Saul, and pick out a few of the lessons which are incidental in his sad story.

First, *advantages are not in themselves a guarantee of success.* Good family connections such as Saul had (ix. 1), fine physique, amiable qualities of disposition—we dare not lean too hard on these. We do not underrate these, of course. If we have had godly fathers, praying mothers, good upbringing, and other such advantages, we can never be too grateful. Yet even these can be a subtle danger. They can beget self-righteousness and pride in us, and a false self-dependence. We may have all these advantages, and yet "play the fool," and perish in the end.

Second, *the greatest opportunities which can come to us are not in themselves enough to give life its highest fulfilment.* Who ever had higher opportunities than Saul? Yet he ended by saying, "I have played the fool." It has been well said that "opportunities do not crown men." You and I may be called to a kingdom, to some high ministry for God, to overseas missionary work, to some other special service or influential position. Golden doors may swing open before us; yet we may still "play the fool," and miss the kingdom, and lose the vision, and end in dark self-frustration, through unsubdued and unsanctified self-will.

Third, *not even do special spiritual equipments in themselves certify ultimate achievement.* They did not in the case of Saul. Alas, we could supplement the story of Saul, in this connection, with other illustrations selected from our own days. We may "preach to others" and yet ourselves become "castaways" in the end! We know some who were once choice and gifted servants of Christ, who have erred through self-will and pierced themselves through with many sorrows. To outward appearance it would seem as though they have "fallen from grace." God alone knows. However staunch our Calvinism may be, we dare not presume. The most gifted and used in spiritual ways may decline through the deceitfulness of an uncrucified self-will, and "play the fool."

Look back again over this story of Saul. A man plays the fool when he neglects his godly friends, as Saul neglected Samuel. A man plays the fool when he goes on enterprises for God before God has sent him, as Saul did. A man plays the fool when he disobeys God even in seemingly small matters, as Saul at first did; for such disobedience nearly always leads on to worse default. A man plays the fool when he trys to cover up his disobedience to God by religious excuses, as Saul did. "To obey is better than sacrifice." A man plays the fool when he tries to persuade himself that he is doing the will of God, as Saul tried to persuade himself, when all the time, deep down in his heart, he knows otherwise. A man plays the fool when he allows some jealousy or hatred to master and enslave and deprave him, as Saul did, towards David. A man plays the fool when he knowingly fights against God, as Saul did in hunting David, to save his own face. A man plays the fool when he turns from God— from the God he has grieved—and seeks an alternative in spiritism, in traffic with spirits in the Beyond. The end of all these ways of sin and folly is moral and spiritual suicide. We can only finish any such downgrade course with the pathetic groan of Saul— *"I have played the fool."*

And now, by way of sharp relief and contrast, look for a moment at that *other* Saul—the Saul of the New Testament. Here, too, is a man of uncommon personal powers and advantages, with a call from God to a vital ministry—though a ministry involving many hazards, and having none of those outward conducements which king Saul's elevation had. What a contrast these two Sauls make! With the Saul of the Old Testament there is progressive downgrade. With the Saul of the New Testament there is progressive upgrade: he presses on for the "prize of the upward calling of God in Christ Jesus." With the Saul of the Old Testament "self" more and more gets the upper hand. With the Saul of the New Testament there is a progressive displacement of self-consciousness by Christ-consciousness. With the self-centred Saul of the Old Testament the personality becomes more and more emaciated. With the Saul of the New Testament the personality becomes more and more sublimated. Instead of being ego-centric, the Saul of the New Testament becomes Christo-centric,—"I live, yet not I, but Christ liveth in me; and the life which I now live in the body, I live by faith in the Son of God, who loved me and gave Himself for me." "To me to live is Christ; and to die is gain." Saul of the New Testament, your name shall be no longer Saul, but Paul; for in a way which was never true of the Old Testament Saul, *you* have indeed become "another man"!

Oh, the contrast! For Saul to live was "self." For Paul to live was "Christ." For Saul to die was shame and gloom. For Paul to die was "gain" and "glory." Both these men drew near to death with the words, "I have . . ." upon their lips; but how different is Saul's "I have" from Paul's! Saul's heart-rending requiem is, "I have played the fool." Paul's martyrdom song is, "I have fought the good fight, I have finished the course, I have kept the faith. Henceforth there is laid up for me the crown . . . !" The Saul of the Old Testament, who lived for self, threw his crown away. The Saul of the New Testament, who lived for Christ, gained a crown which will never lose its lustre through all the ages! God help us to read, mark, and learn!

> Live for self, you live in vain;
> Live for Christ, you live again;
> Live for Him, with Him you reign—
> "HENCEFORTH, THE CROWN"!

THE MAN WHO BORE THE BRANDS

SCRIPTURE SNAPSHOT

See with how large letters I have written unto you with mine own hand. As many as desire to make a fair show in the flesh, they compel you to be circumcised, only that they may not be persecuted for the cross of Christ. For not even they who receive circumcision do themselves keep the law ; but they desire to have you circumcised, that they may glory in your flesh. But far be it from me to glory, save in the cross of our Lord Jesus Christ, through which the world hath been crucified unto me, and I unto the world. For neither is circumcision anything, nor uncircumcision, but a new creature. And as many as shall walk by this rule, peace be unto them, and mercy, and upon the Israel of God.

From henceforth let no man trouble me : for I bear branded on my body the marks of Jesus.

The grace of our Lord Jesus Christ be with your spirit, brethren. Amen.—Galatians vi. 11–18 (R.V.).

THE MAN WHO BORE THE BRANDS

*"From henceforth let no man trouble me: for I bear
in my body the marks of the Lord Jesus."*

—Galatians vi. 17.

"THE MARKS of the Lord Jesus"—what were they? The Greek
word which is here translated as "marks" is *stigmata,* from which
we get our English words "stigma" and "stigmatise." The Revised
Version gives its English sense more clearly by translating it as
"I bear *branded* on my body the marks of the Lord Jesus."

It is quite clear that the apostle is here referring to actual
marks which he bore in his body; yet his use of that word
stigmata to describe them makes it equally clear that he was
giving to these marks a kind of figurative or symbolic meaning.
They were not *merely* marks: they were brands; and in calling
them such Paul was evidently alluding to some practice of branding, or flesh-marking, which would be well-known to his Galatian
readers.

This gives rise to two questions: What was the branding to
which Paul here figuratively alludes? and what were the actual
marks on his body?

WHAT WAS THE BRANDING?

First, then, what was the branding to which Paul here figuratively alludes? There seem to have been *five* classes of persons
who were branded. It was a common thing in olden times to
brand *slaves,* the brand being a mark of ownership, or a means
of precaution against running away, or even a mode of punishment. There is a Scriptural example of slave-branding given in
Exodus xxi. 5–6: "And if the servant shall plainly say, I love
my master, my wife, and my children; I will not go out free:

then his master shall bring him unto the judges; he shall also bring him to the door, or unto the door post; and his master shall bore his ear through with an aul; and he shall serve him for ever." The main idea, then, in slave-branding was *ownership*.

But besides being used among slaves, branding was also common among *soldiers*. Then, as in more recent times, soldiers tattooed on their arm or hand the name or initials of favourite generals, as, for instance, the soldiers of Alexander the Great, who bore his Alpha on their flesh. Vegetius, writing three hundred years later than Paul's time, tells us that in the Roman Army raw recruits had to be proved fit for service by stiff trial before they were allowed to have the tattoo put upon them. The main idea in the branding of the soldier is that of *allegiance*.

But again, religious *devotees* were often branded. Their consecration to old-time gods was frequently signalised by "stigmata." For instance, Herodotus, writing a long while before Paul, says about one of Heracles' temples on the Egyptian coast, that if a servant belonging to any man resorted to it for sanctuary, and became sealed with the sacred stigmata, thus giving himself up to the god, none could touch him. There seems to be an allusion to this practice of devotional branding in Isaiah xliv. 5, where the words: "Another shall subscribe with his hand unto the Lord" should read: "Another shall *inscribe on his hand*: I am Jehovah's" (see R.V. Margin).

Still further, we find that stigmata were inflicted upon *criminals*. Persons of a vile or dangerous character were sometimes branded so that their identity might be open to immediate detection, and their infamy become patent to all. It is from such usages as this that the word *stigmata* came to have the unhappy meaning that still clings to it in our English word "stigma," which comes from it. This kind of branding reaches right back to the dawn of human history; for Cain, the first man ever born to a human mother, committed fratricide, and was branded by God Himself.

Once more, stigmata were sometimes inflicted upon *the abhorred,* as a mark of approbrium and insult. In one of the books of the Apocrypha—the third book of the Maccabees, chapter ii. 29—we are told that Philopater caused the Jews to be "marked on their persons" by the ivy-leaf symbol of the

Greek god Dionysus, which branding we are told was intended "to inflict a public stigma" on the abhorred Jewish race, and was effected by means of fire.

These, then, were the five classes subject to branding,—the slave, the soldier, the devotee, the criminal, the abhorred; and these are the five meanings of the brandings,—on the slave, a mark of ownership; on the soldier, a mark of allegiance; on the devotee, a mark of consecration; on the criminal, a mark of exposure; on the abhorred, a mark of reproach.

Now certain commentators on Galatians go to considerable pains to decide which class of branding Paul had in mind when he said "I bear in my body the *stigmata* of the Lord Jesus,"— whether the branding of the slave, or of the soldier, or of some other. But surely this is needless. Paul was alluding to brand-marks *generally*, just as someone to-day might use the metaphor: "I wear the *uniform* of a Christian," without meaning in particular the uniform of a soldier, or of a chauffeur, or of a civil attendant, or of a corporation employee, but uniform comprehensively.

The "brand-marks of the Lord Jesus" on the person of Paul were those of all five classes. They were the brand-marks of the slave; for they sealed Christ's *ownership* of Paul. They were the brand-marks of the soldier; for they proclaimed Paul's *allegiance* to his heavenly Captain. They were the brand-marks of the devotee; for they declared Paul's *consecration* to his Divine Lord. They were even the brand-marks of the criminal, for they disfigured him into unmistakable *identification* as the apostle of the Nazarene. They were also the brand-marks of the abhorred; for they had been largely inflicted as an expression of *abhorrence* by Jewish adversaries of the Gospel.

WHAT WERE THE MARKS?

And now we ask: What were the *actual marks* on Paul's body, which he here speaks of as "brands"? There can be no doubt about the answer. They were those scars and sears and, maybe, long-continuing sores which had come upon him during his costly and heroic service for the sake of Christ and the

Gospel. The hardship and ill-usage which he had undergone had taken their toll and left their marks; and these pathetic disfigurements must have told with a sad eloquence of the way in which Paul's fellow-men regarded him and treated him.

That Paul was meaning these physical injuries, when he said "I bear in my body the brand-marks of the Lord Jesus," is borne out by the fact that about the same time he mentioned them in writing to the Corinthians. In his second epistle to the Corinthians, chapter xi. 23–28, he breaks out with the following pathetic and passionate reminder—"In labours more abundant, in stripes above measure, in prisons more frequent, in deaths oft. Of the Jews five times I received forty stripes save one. Thrice was I beaten with rods, once was I stoned, thrice I suffered shipwreck, a night and a day I have been in the deep; in journeyings often, in perils of waters, in perils of robbers, in perils by mine own countrymen, in perils by the heathen, in perils in the city, in perils in the wilderness, in perils in the sea, in perils among false brethren; in weariness and painfulness, in watchings often, in hunger and thirst, in fastings often, in cold and nakedness. Beside those things that are without, that which cometh upon me daily, the care of all the churches."

It may be that about the time of his writing to the Galatians he had been going through further painful experiences from which he was still suffering, and which drew his mind to speak of all his other sufferings and the toll which they had exacted. Ah, yes, Paul had been battered and bruised in ways which could not but leave permanent memorials on his poor body. Could he, for instance, have undergone that stoning at Lystra—after which he was dragged outside the city and left for dead—without bearing life-long after-effects?

We do not know whether his five Jewish whippings would leave any abiding marks; but the three floggings by the Roman soldiers would plough lines which would remain for life. And besides this, there were those more barbarous violences which he suffered by the brutality of mobs, the ambush of enemies, the assaults of robbers, and such like. Such had been his bodily hardships, and such must have been the effects, that by his appearance he would be easily taken to be some deservedly wretched outcast paying the penalty of his criminality. Indeed, the apostle himself, in 1 Corinthians iv. 9–13, speaks of himself as being treated thus—"For I think that God hath set forth us apostles last, as it were appointed to death: for we are made a spectacle unto the world, and to angels, and to men. We are fools for Christ's sake. Even unto this present hour we both hunger and thirst, and are naked, and are buffeted, and have no certain dwellingplace; and labour, working with our own hands; being reviled we bless; being persecuted, we suffer it: being defamed, we intreat: we are made as the filth of the world, and are the offscouring of all things unto this day."

These then were the marks on Paul's body—the marks of his service and suffering for Christ's sake, for the Galatians' sake, and for our own sake who reap such precious harvest from his labours; and Paul calls them "the brand-marks of the Lord Jesus."

WHY ARE THE STIGMATA MENTIONED?

And now, I have two further questions to ask. First, why does Paul refer to these "brand-marks" in this context? Second, how do these "brand-marks" of Paul concern you and me?

First, then, why does Paul refer to these "brand-marks" in this context?

One clear reason is indicated by the fact that in the Greek here the pronoun "I" is emphatic. Read the words again, emphasizing that pronoun—"*I* bear in my body the brands of the Lord Jesus." Paul emphasizes the personal pronoun here to mark a contrast between himself and the Judaizing teachers who were subverting the Galatian believers and seeking to turn them against himself. These self-important men were mouthing big pretensions; but did *they* bear the brand-marks of the Lord Jesus in their persons, as Paul did? No; like most shouters they were shirkers. They were swell preachers but poor sufferers. They had a profound regard for the safety of their own skin. They were fine platform figures, but they dreaded persecution for the sake of the Cross. Mark it well—the real test of our love to Christ is what we are prepared to *suffer* for Him. Let us not make big professions if we are not prepared to seal them with our blood.

A second reason why Paul here speaks of these brand-marks is found in his emphasis on the fact that they are "the brands of the Lord *Jesus.*" He is drawing a contrast between the marks of *Jesus* and that of *Moses.* See verses 12 to 15. "As many as desire to make a fair show in the flesh, they constrain you to be circumcised; only lest they should suffer persecution for the cross of Christ"—and so on. The Judaizing teachers who were misleading the Galatian converts were telling them that they must undergo the rite of circumcision. Paul stoutly repudiates this teaching. Circumcision is the mark of *Moses,* and speaks of servitude to a legal system from the curse of which the Lord Jesus, by His redeeming death and resurrection, has set us free. It is not the mark of Moses, but the marks of the Lord Jesus that the Christian is to bear. The mark of Moses is that of a binding ritual. The marks of the Lord Jesus are those of a glad, free, self-sacrificing service. Over against these legalistic preachers who were undermining the faith of the Galatians, Paul glories that as for himself, he bears in *his* body, not merely the mark of Moses, but "the marks of the Lord Jesus."

A third reason why Paul here refers to these brand-marks is found in the words, *"From henceforth let no man trouble me."* This epistle is full of trouble. The Galatians had been troubled; and Paul had just written: "I would they were even cut off which trouble you." Paul himself had been troubled. He speaks of "travailing in birth again" as regards his Galatian children. And all the trouble came from these Judaistic fifth-columnists who were bent on perverting the young faith of Paul's converts to Christ. But these false teachers were also *attacking Paul himself,* were questioning his sincerity and discrediting his apostleship. The one trouble was bad enough; but that the battle-scarred Paul should himself still continue to be thus personally maligned and sinisterly doubted was almost more than the gallant apostle could endure. And in the words: "From henceforth let no man trouble me, for I bear in my body the brands of the Lord Jesus," there is something of touching appeal, that if these subversive teachers have any sense of honour or honesty at all they will at least drop this dastardly trick of destroying faith in Paul's own sincerity, seeing that he had now suffered so much for the message which he preached. Paul felt—and rightly so—that he had received enough scars to place his loyalty, as Christ's servant and apostle, beyond doubt. The very name of Jesus, so to speak, had become branded up and down his bruised and buffeted body. Henceforth, therefore, let not men perpetuate the cruelty of raising doubts about his relationship to his Master. "From henceforth let no man trouble me, for (to settle any doubts as to sincerity) I bear in my very body, the brand-marks of the Lord Jesus."

THE STIGMATA AND OURSELVES

Finally, how do these brand-marks of Paul concern ourselves?

Well, first they tell us that *we should never be ashamed of bearing suffering or reproach for Jesus' sake.* The most honoured of the apostles regarded himself as the branded slave of Christ. He could not have got lower; and he could not have climbed higher. He knew no higher honour than to be such. He gloried in it, as the context tells us. Let us never forget that real Christianity is living for Christ instead of for self; and let us be like those early Christians who "departed from the presence of the Council, rejoicing that they were counted worthy to suffer shame for the Name." There can be no higher honour than to suffer for Him who so sublimely suffered for us, that we might become eternally saved.

> Captain beloved, battle wounds were Thine,
> Let me not wonder if some hurt be mine,
> Rather, O Lord, let my deep wonder be,
> That I may share a battle wound with Thee.

Second, the brand-marks of Paul tell us that *we should not be afraid of bearing such marks in our own bodies.* Far better be scarred than scared. When John Knox came back from the French galleys, his hands were marked by the oar to which he had been chained for eighteen months. What those hands spoke! Young Mrs. Knox, overcome, knelt and kissed them. An authoress who once dined with Mary Slessor, the heroic Calabar missionary, wrote about Mary's hands: "They were hardened and roughened by work in the past, and they were bleeding from work finished but now; the skin of the palms was gone; the nails were worn to the quick: that they were painful there could be no doubt, but she only apologised for their appearance." What sacrificial toil of love those hands spoke! Let us never be afraid of such *stigmata* for the Saviour's sake. Nor let us fear persecution or ridicule or trial; for these things help to burn in us "the marks of the Lord Jesus."

Yet again, Paul's brand-marks suggest that *we should bear the marks of the Lord Jesus in our character*. We may not all be called upon to bear marks of cruelty upon our bodies, but we are all called to bear the marks of the indwelling Christ upon our *character*. It is said that Saint Francis of Assisi bore literally in his hands the marks of crucifixion—the reproduction of Christ's own wounds, and that these came after one of the saint's protracted seasons of prayer. It is said, also, that he carried these marks to the day of his death. How they came to be there is an unsolved mystery; and we find it difficult to exercise too much credence. But this is certain, that in a moral and spiritual sense the marks of Jesus ought to be reproduced in each of His people —His holiness and love and grace and meekness and His self-sacrificing willingness for service. We should bear the marks that speak of the willing slave, of the loyal soldier, of the earnest devotee—the marks that speak of ownership and allegiance and consecration. Oh that we may bear such marks!

Finally, if we bear such marks, we may pass at last from earth to heaven as Paul did, exclaiming: "I am now ready to be offered, and the time of my departure is at hand. I have fought the good fight; I have finished the course; I have kept the faith. Henceforth there is laid up for me a crown of righteousness, which the Lord, the righteous Judge, shall give me at that day; and not to me only, but unto all them that love His appearing"! May it indeed be so!

THE MAN WHO BRAVED THE LIONS

SCRIPTURE SNAPSHOT

Then they came near, and spake before the king concerning the king's interdict: Hast thou not signed an interdict, that every man that shall make petition unto any god or man within thirty days, save unto thee, O king, shall be cast into the den of lions? The king answered and said, The thing is true, according to the law of the Medes and Persians, which altereth not. Then answered they and said before the king, That Daniel which is of the children of the captivity of Judah, regardeth not thee, O king, nor the interdict that thou hast signed, but maketh his petition three times a day. Then the king, when he heard these words, was sore displeased, and set his heart on Daniel to deliver him: and he laboured till the going down of the sun to rescue him. Then these men assembled together unto the king, and said unto the king, Know, O king, that it is a law of the Medes and Persians, that no interdict nor statute which the king establisheth may be changed. Then the king commanded, and they brought Daniel, and cast him into the den of lions. Now the king spake and said unto Daniel, Thy God whom thou servest continually, he will deliver thee. And a stone was brought, and laid upon the mouth of the den; and the king sealed it with his own signet, and with the signet of his lords; that nothing might be changed concerning Daniel.

Then the king went to his palace, and passed the night fasting; neither were instruments of music brought before him; and his sleep fled from him. Then the king arose very early in the morning, and went in haste unto the den of lions. And when he came near unto the den to Daniel, he cried with a lamentable voice: the king spake and said to Daniel, O Daniel, servant of the living God, is thy God, whom thou servest continually, able to deliver thee from the lions? Then said Daniel unto the king, O king, live for ever. My God hath sent his angel, and hath shut the lions' mouths, and they have not hurt me; forasmuch as before him, innocency was found in me; and also before thee, O king, have I done no hurt. Then was the king exceeding glad, and commanded that they should take Daniel up out of the den. So Daniel was taken up out of the den, and no manner of hurt was found upon him, because he had trusted in his God.—Daniel vi. 12–23 (R.V.).

THE MAN WHO BRAVED THE LIONS

"No manner of hurt was found upon him, because he believed in his God."—Daniel vi. 23.

THE SIMPLE, obvious lesson in these words is that faith in God is the best protection. "No manner of hurt was found upon him, because he believed in his God." Had Daniel trusted in anything or anyone else he would certainly have perished; but because he made God his confidence he was delivered. This gives us much comfort to-day; for although times have greatly changed since Daniel was on earth, Daniel's God has not changed; and it is still true that they who make God their confidence shall not be ashamed.

This matter of faith in God gets right down to the roots of life; and the peculiar tendencies of our day are such as to suggest that we need to re-examine and re-establish our acceptance of this dogma that faith in God, really and honestly, *is* our highest wisdom and truest safety. We are encircled to-day by a ring of teachers who would assure us that faith in God, as a principle by which to live, is the obsolete conception of an unscientific, unenlightened, and credulous day which is now past.

Some of our leading *psychologists* and their satellites are quite sure that the great thing now is faith in one's own self, the building up of a "superiority complex" which crowns itself in the satisfaction of achievement through self-realisation. Then there are those among our more philosophically-minded *biologists* who would have us put our faith in humanity as a species. Through the lapse of millenniums man has been steadily climbing to higher things, until such is the point of development reached to-day, and so accelerated is man's evolution now, that if only we will have faith in humanity and help on the movement of progress, we shall comparatively soon arrive at the "happy ever after" stage. Yes, they are still bravely preaching this upward progress of man, despite the millions of "missing links," and despite the most depraved and brutal and blood-curdling war of all history! Yes, they are still preaching it, the poor, proud, educated sillies —for they will believe even in bubbles rather than in God!

Then again, there are the *nationalists* and *militarists* who would have us live our life on a purely physical basis, putting our faith in physical power. They preach the Gospel of a "national consciousness" expressing itself through the "Totalitarian State." After all, what do we know about the Beyond or the spiritual? Why bother our heads about metaphysical mysteries? Let us put our faith in that which is concrete, and we shall find in the end that "might is right."

Of course we may reply to the *psychologist* that there are deeper depths of yearning in the human heart than any line of psychology has ever plumbed. Faith in our own selves is a poor pillow to lay our weary heads upon when sickness and poverty and sorrow and cruel frustrations have left us bruised and fevered. At such times, you find that psychology is no balm of Gilead, and your "superiority complex" is just about as comforting as an iceberg. We may remind the *biologist* who would have us put our faith in total humanity that each human heart is far more alive to its own separate existence and needs than it is to any vague "race-consciousness." Faith in humanity as such leaves the pressing, ever-present problems of the individual coldly untouched. We may also rebut the *militarist* by the unhesitating reply that the deepest and truest longings of the human heart are not for the mere physical protection which he precariously offers, but for a sense of *spiritual* security. When a soul is really awakened to a realization of sin before God, to the terror of death, and judgment and eternal ruin, it is not protection even from the atomic bomb which it cries for, but salvation from *sin*! As we think of some among our new would-be teachers, the old lines in "Hamlet" come to mind:

> There are more things in heaven and earth, Horatio,
> Than are dreamt of in your philosophy.

It is not our purpose here, however, to enter the lists in combative argument against these groups: they are mentioned, rather, to show that there is indeed good reason to-day for us to ground ourselves firmly in the great old truth that the truest wisdom and best security is *faith in God*. It is this that our text brings home again to us: "No manner of hurt was found upon him, because he believed in his God." Let us think then of (1) Daniel's faith in God—"He believed in his God," and (2) God's care of Daniel— "No manner of hurt was found upon him."

DANIEL'S FAITH IN GOD

It goes almost without saying that the words: "He believed in his God" mean much more than any bare assent to the fact of God's existence. Such a belief in God as Daniel had is a thing far more of the heart than merely of the head. He "believed in his God" in the sense of sincere trust,—living in dependence on Him, relying on Him for salvation and preservation, and for vindication against the ungodly. I hope that you, too, have this kind of belief in God, that you are truly relying on Him for forgiveness and cleansing and guidance and keeping-power and eternal salvation through the Lord Jesus Christ. This kind of believing saves our souls; it has a regenerating power, and makes our life on earth a noble, worthwhile thing.

Now there are four prominent features about Daniel's faith which capture our attention; and the first of these is its *clarity*. There was a lot of vagueness about in Daniel's day, even as there is in our own time. The original religious faith of his nation had been muddied by a mix-up with the superstitious, idolatrous systems of other peoples. But Daniel's own faith in God was marked by clarity. He was clear about God's wisdom, as we see in connection with the king's dream. He was clear about God's sovereignty and foreknowledge, as we see in his interpretation of the Image. He was clear about God's holiness and almightiness and faithfulness, as we see again and again in reading the book. Where did he get all this clear knowledge? He got it from the Scriptures, together with first-hand experience of God's dealings. He was a man who "knew what he believed and why he believed it." What a need there is for such clear-cut faith to-day! If we have a clear faith like that of Daniel's we may be spiritual guides and leaders to the people of our day, even as Daniel was to those people in the long ago: and if we would have such a clear, intelligent faith, we must get to know the God of the Bible. To all young people I would say: Let this great book be your life-long teacher! Someone has well said that we should "*know* it in the head; *stow* it in the heart; *show* it in the life; *sow* it in the world." Bishop Ryle was right in saying that, as a result of our having the Bible, the young scholars in our Sunday School know more clear truth about Divine things than Socrates and Plato and the other Greek philosophers knew through all their philosophies. If we would have a clear faith like Daniel's we must know God's Book.

The second quality in Daniel's faith was that of *loyalty*. Daniel lived at a time when the true faith was unpopular and many people were proving disloyal to the old standards. It was this disloyal break-away from Israel's true faith which had brought calamity to Daniel's nation, just as the modern break-away from the Word of God is responsible more than anything else for the troubles that have recently come upon Europe and have involved the whole world. But amid the surrounding failure of belief, young man Daniel remained loyal. Oh for more Daniels to-day! Young people, don't just be Sunday Christians, afraid to stand up loyally for Jesus during the week. Don't be a wax-work disciple,—all wax but no work! Don't sing "Stand up, stand up for Jesus, ye soldiers of the Cross," and then scamper away at the first rifle-crack from the enemy lines! It is hard to be a loyal Christian; that is one of the reasons why it is *grand*!

> Dare to be a Daniel,
>   Dare to stand alone;
> Dare to have a purpose firm,
>   And dare to make it known.

The third thing about Daniel's faith was its *fixity*. Despite the king's decree forbidding religious freedom and threatening banishment to that "concentration camp" of the lions, Daniel Niemoller remained resolute. Until quite recently, critics of the

Bible have scorned to believe that there ever was any such thing as a "den of lions" in old-time Babylon; but it is now discovered that it was a common thing for old-time cities to have such a den as that to which Daniel was committed, and such a furnace as that into which Shadrach, Meshach, and Abed-nego were cast, —and they were kept for purposes of punishment. Such discoveries are part of the great service which Archæology is rendering to the Bible in our own wonderful day. Yes, the lion's den was real enough! Yet Daniel was not deterred. "He believed in his God"! There seemed no way of escape apart from compromise; but to a man of Daniel's faith death was far better than compromise! He would be true to his God whatever the consequences,—like the young man who gave up his wealth and high position that he might preach Christ to the cannibals, and then went forth with this motto: "The will of God, nothing less, nothing more, nothing else,—*at all costs*!" There is a modern Daniel in Germany, of whom we have heard much recently. Dr. Niemoller of Germany had to endure long months of imprisonment because he refused to put the State before his God. When Dr. Niemoller was interned, the prison chaplain asked him: "Why are you in prison, brother?"—and Dr. Niemoller answered: "Why are *you not* in prison, brother?" Yes, indeed, Jesus needs the bravest and noblest that is in us! Let us stand fast and firm for Him!

The fourth thing about Daniel's faith was its *certainty*. It says that Daniel "believed in *his* God." He was Daniel's God by outward profession and inward conversion. He was Daniel's God by a first-hand experience. He was Daniel's God because He had revealed a special interest in Daniel, and a special plan for his life. Can each of ourselves say: "This God is *my* God?" Can each of us say, "Jesus is *my* Saviour,—mine both by outward profession and by inward conversion, by a first-hand experience, and because I know He has a real plan for my life"? Some of our scientists tell us to-day that the only things which we really know are those things which we have experienced. Certainly, when we have experienced a thing, we cannot longer doubt it. Ah, it is a great thing to have this kind of certainty about God, about Christ, about salvation! I pray that we all may know God in this way. "Daniel believed in *his* God."

GOD'S CARE OF DANIEL

Let us now see God's care of Daniel,—"*No manner of hurt was found upon him.*" There are four things which impress us about Daniel's preservation. The first of these is its *miraculousness.* Never had there been a tastier morsel in that lion's den than well-favoured Daniel; yet "no manner of hurt was found upon him!" And *why* did not the lions demolish Daniel? The answer to that question is given by Daniel himself: "My God hath sent His angel, and hath shut the lions' mouths." I am quite sure that those lions had never suffered from such a strange lock-jaw before! God had intervened in this miraculous way to vindicate Daniel; and thus "no manner of hurt was found upon him."

Yes, this intervention to save Daniel falls into the category of what we call the "miraculous"; and it is well to see it in its historical context. Those who lived in Daniel's time did not have the revelation of God in Christ, or the completed Scriptures, which we ourselves have. It was necessary, therefore, that God should teach them in ways suited to their stage of development in the apprehension of spiritual truths. Vivid objects and miraculous interventions were frequently used for this purpose. The need for these is not the same to-day. God could just as easily intervene by such miracles of a physical kind to-day; but that method of dealing is now largely superseded by the fuller light of revelation which is ours. Of course, it is true *to-day* that in answer to prayer God heals the sick, sends rain, opens up employment, and sends money to the needy: yet speaking generally, God's present method is to work through normal channels.

This change of dispensation and of general method does not in the least impair the truth that God has the ways and means of delivering His Daniels to-day just as truly as ever in olden times; so that it is still true to say with the psalmist: "None of them that trust in Him shall be desolate."

Another thing which strikes us about Daniel's deliverance is its *instructiveness.* God did not save Daniel from being *put into* the lions' den; but He saved Him *in* it, and brought him through the ordeal without any manner of hurt being found upon him. Faith was tried and tested, but it was also honoured and vindicated. Very often our prayers are that we might escape trials and testing; but we know not what we are asking. The word of God gives no guarantee that Christ's people shall be immune from trials and testings. On the contrary, it indicates that they may suffer the more. Yet there is the unfailing guarantee that faith in Christ will never fail to be honoured. God allows His Daniels to be put into the den; but He sends His angel and preserves them. He allows His jewels to be put on the lapidary's wheel, but it is that they may become the more beautiful. He does not save us *from*; but He saves us *in,* and brings us *through.*

Thirdly, and mainly, see the completeness of Daniel's preservation: *"No manner* of hurt was found upon him." I remember hearing Dr. Henry Montgomery of Belfast humorously remark that when Darius the king called aloud to Daniel in the den, to learn if he had survived, Daniel replied that the lions had not even "chewed a button off!"

But here we encounter an objection. Someone says: "It may be true that 'no manner of hurt' was found upon Daniel; but there are thousands and thousands of others who have trusted God, and who *have* suffered hurt, despite their faith—and have suffered severely too. What about those who, although their faith in God has been like that of Daniel's, have suffered martyrdom? How can it be said of such that 'no manner of hurt' was found upon them because they trusted in their God? What about Christian missionaries who have gone forth in faith, yet have succumbed to fever and other maladies in tropical climates? What about Christian businessmen who, despite their integrity and faith in God, have been allowed to suffer bankruptcy? What about all these and the countless other instances of suffering and calamity among the Lord's faithful servants? How can you say of these that 'no manner of hurt' was found upon them? And if you *cannot* say that they were delivered as Daniel was, what then of God's promised protection?"

The answer to this objection is twofold. First, God has not promised always to give protection either from physical or mental adversity. There is a higher form of protection than that. Very often, strange though it may sound, the physical and mental adversity are necessary to make real this higher form of protection. Which was the greater triumph of faith in God—David's slaying of Goliath, with a sling, or martyred Stephen's crying out, as he sank beneath the pelting stones, "Lord, lay not this sin to their charge"? In the one case *physical* victory and deliverance were given. In the other case the victory and deliverance were *spiritual*. We certainly could not say of Stephen, that no manner of *physical* hurt was found upon him: yet how truly and gloriously may the words of our text be used of him in a *spiritual* sense! "No manner of hurt was found upon him, despite all the evil rage of his murderers, because he trusted in his God." And what was true in the case of Stephen the martyr is true of all those other Daniels and Stephens who, through good and ill, through laughter and tears, in living and in dying, have believed in their God. No sickness, no adversity, no enemy can do them real harm; and when at last they rise to their inheritance in heaven, the angels crowd around them, and bless the God of heaven while they say one to another: "No manner of hurt is found on them, because they believed in their God."

But the greatest demonstration of the fact that no manner of hurt comes upon any of God's Daniels is that which will be seen in the consummation yet to be. When the Lord Jesus returns in glory, to set up His millennial kingdom, those who have suffered for Him will reign with Him; and then it will be seen by all, that "no manner of hurt" is found on them. The twentieth chapter of Revelation speaks about this. It says: "And I saw thrones, and them that sat upon them, and judgment was given unto them. And I saw the souls of them that were beheaded for the witness of Jesus and for the word of God . . . *and they lived and reigned with Christ the thousand years!*"

That consecrated young man who went out to be a missionary, and was martyred at the age of thirty, thus cutting his life on earth short by forty or even fifty years, is thus compensated by twenty times the forfeited years; for he "lives and reigns" on earth with Christ, throughout the Millennium! Those worldly-wise men and women who said he was throwing his life and gifts away in becoming a poor missionary, now stand confounded as they see him in his resurrection beauty and splendour. He lives again! That poor body which was battered to the grave has now come forth a glorious body, fashioned after the likeness of Christ Himself. It is an immortal, incorruptible, indescribably wonderful and beautiful body which irradiates a supernal glory. No spot or wrinkle or any such thing even slightly disfigures it. See him then—that resurrected and raptured martyr—as he lives and reigns with Christ in millennial glory. "No manner of hurt is found upon him, because he believed in his God!" Yes, see him, amid all the bloom and beauty of that coming Springtime and let him tell you that it will at last be said about *all* of God's Daniels: "No manner of hurt was found upon them because they believed in their God."

Finally, see the *convincingness* of Daniel's deliverance. When Daniel came back from that lion's den, and Darius actually saw that "no manner of hurt was found upon him, because he believed in his God," he became absolutely convinced that Daniel's God was the one true God who ruled over all. Indeed, I think we may say even more than that. Darius, who sat on the mightiest throne of his day, became *converted* to the true God; for he issued the following decree, to be published in all the realms of Media-Persia:

"Peace be multiplied unto you. I make a decree: That in every dominion of my kingdom men tremble and fear before the God of Daniel: for He is the living God, and steadfast for ever, and His kingdom that which shall not be destroyed, and His dominion shall be even unto the end. He delivereth and rescueth, and He worketh signs and wonders in heaven and in earth, who hath delivered Daniel from the power of the lions."

As we see Daniel being turned into that den of lions, we cannot but exclaim: *"What an ordeal!"* But as we see Darius publishing that edict to "all people, nations, and languages, that dwell in all the earth," we cannot but exclaim: *"What a sequel!"* We never know what great thing may come of it if we stand firm in our faith despite temptation and persecution and adversity. The eyes of men are upon us; and if we are true to our faith God will certainly bless our witness for Him. Let us resolve, then, that by the aid of the Holy Spirit we too will trust God as Daniel did; and in the end, beyond the shadow of a doubt, it will be said, even of us: "No manner of hurt was found upon them, because they believed in their God."

THE MAN WHO CURSED THE CHILDREN

SCRIPTURE SNAPSHOT

ELISHA AT JORDAN

And it came to pass, as they still went on, and talked, that, behold, there appeared a chariot of fire, and horses of fire, which parted them both asunder ; and Elijah went up by a whirlwind into heaven. And Elisha saw it, and he cried, My father, my father, the chariots of Israel and the horsemen thereof ! And he saw him no more ; and he took hold of his own clothes, and rent them in two pieces. He took up also the mantle of Elijah that fell from him, and went back, and stood by the bank of Jordan. And he took the mantle of Elijah that fell from him, and smote the waters, and said, Where is the Lord, the God of Elijah ? and when he also had smitten the waters, they were divided hither and thither ; and Elisha went over. And when the sons of the prophets which were at Jericho over against him saw him, they said, The spirit of Elijah doth rest on Elisha.

ELISHA AT JERICHO

And the men of the city said unto Elisha, Behold, we pray thee, the situation of this city is pleasant, as my lord seeth ; but the water is naught, and the land miscarrieth. And he said, Bring me a new cruse, and put salt therein. And they brought it to him. And he went forth unto the spring of the waters, and cast salt therein, and said, Thus saith the Lord, I have healed these waters ; there shall not be from thence any more death or miscarrying. So the waters were healed unto this day, according to the word of Elisha which he spake.

ELISHA AT BETHEL

And he went up from thence unto Beth-el ; and as he was going up by the way there came forth little children out of the city, and mocked him, and said unto him, Go up, thou bald head ; go up, thou bald head. And he looked behind him and saw them, and cursed them in the name of the Lord. And there came forth two she-bears out of the wood, and tare forty and two children of them. And he went from thence to mount Carmel, and from thence he returned to Samaria.—2 Kings ii. 11–25 (R.V.).

THE MAN WHO CURSED THE CHILDREN

"And he (Elisha) went up from thence unto Beth-el: and as he was going up by the way, there came forth little children out of the city, and mocked him, and said unto him, Go up, thou bald head; go up, thou bald head. And he turned back, and looked on them, and cursed them in the name of the Lord. And there came forth two she-bears out of the wood, and tare forty and two children of them."—2 Kings ii. 23, 24.

PERHAPS no incident in the Old Testament has called forth more criticism than this one. The Lord's enemies have held it up as a trump card in their pack of arguments against the claim of the Bible to be the word of God. A young University graduate recently told a friend of mine that this incident alone was enough to turn him against the Bible. How could we possibly believe that God would send bears to devour little children, just to satisfy the spite of a man who was riled by their innocent banter? Surely it is bad taste for the Bible even to preserve such a fiction, for the spirit here shown by Elisha is peevish in the extreme; but that the Bible should actually palm the thing off as *true*, and have us believe that God acted in this way toward these little folk, that in itself is enough to discredit the whole Bible! We cannot put confidence in such a book.

Well, such cheap criticisms of the Bible are usually the fulsome garblings of ignorance, or the shifty device of prejudice. Certainly, in the case of the incident before us, a little patient investigating of the Biblical narrative knocks the bottom out of such cavilling. Let us look into the incident a little more closely. We will try to *explain* it and then to *apply* it.

BY WAY OF EXPLANATION

We need to be clear about three factors: (i) the offenders; (ii) the offence; (iii) the punishment.

First, then, who were the *offenders*? Our English translation says they were "little children"; but in a case like this we must go back beyond our English version to the Hebrew original. The two Hebrew words which our English version gives as "little children" are *qatan* and *na'ar*. Take first the one which is translated as "children" (plural of *na'ar*). In Genesis xxii. 3–5 it is used of the young men whom aged Abraham took with him when he went to sacrifice Isaac. It is also used of Isaac himself, in the same chapter (verse 5, where it is translated "lad"). Now, Isaac is usually reckoned to have been about twenty-two at this time, and the accompanying young fellows would probably be Isaac's seniors by some years. The same word is also used of Ishmael, in Genesis xxi. 12, where it is translated "lad": and we know that Ishmael was then at least sixteen, for he was fourteen when Isaac was born, which was two years or more earlier. It is also used of Joseph, in Genesis xxxii. 2, where it is translated "lad"; and at this time Joseph was twenty-eight: and in Genesis xliv. 31 it is used of Benjamin who must at that time have been well over thirty, and possibly nearer forty. In 1 Kings xx. 14 it is used of the soldiers who routed the Syrians. So that we are easily within bounds when we say that this word might be appropriately used of anybody up to thirty years of age.

Now look at the other word (*qatan*), which is translated as "little" in the Elisha incident. It comes in Genesis xxvii. 42, where it is translated by our English word "younger," and is applied to Jacob at the time when he fled from his brother Esau— at which time he must have been at least in his sixties. It comes again in Genesis xliv. 20, where it is used of Benjamin, who was then in his thirties. It comes again in Judges i. 13, where it is again translated by our English word "younger," and is used of Kenaz, Caleb's younger brother, who must have been over sixty; for he had a grown son at the time, who was old enough and strong enough to storm and capture Kirjath-sepher. It is used in 1 Chronicles xxiv. 31 of the younger priests and Levites, all of whom were grown men (for by the law they were not eligible even to be numbered among their brethren before they were twenty).

It is quite clear, then, without our citing further occurrences of these two Hebrew words, that they are both characterised by considerable elasticity. But besides this, there are places where the two words actually occur together, as they do in this Elisha incident. In 1 Samuel xx. 35 they are used of the youth who fetched Jonathan's arrows when he gave the secret sign to David to flee from Saul. The context makes it quite clear that this "little lad" (as the words are translated) was no little lad at all, but a young fellow. A "little lad" could not have been entrusted with so delicate and important a matter. The two words occur together again in 1 Kings xi. 17, where they are used of Hadad, who (despite the A.V. translation, "little child") was old enough to flee with some of his father's servants to Egypt.

But note most of all 1 Samuel xvi. 11: "And Samuel said unto Jesse: Are here all thy children? And he (Jesse) said: There remaineth yet the youngest (child), and behold he keepeth the sheep. And Samuel said unto Jesse: Send and fetch him; for we will not sit down till he come hither. And he sent, and brought him in. Now he was ruddy, and, withal, of a beautiful countenance, and goodly to look to. And the Lord said: Arise, anoint him; for this is he. Then Samuel took the horn of oil, and anointed him in the midst of his brethren: and the Spirit of the Lord came upon David from that day forward." Now here David is called the *"youngest"* of Jesse's *"children"*; and these are the very two words, in the Hebrew, which are translated as "little children" in the Elisha incident. Yet what was David's age when he was thus described? In verse 18 of the same chapter he is described as being at this very time "a mighty, valiant man, and a man of war, and prudent in matters, and a comely person, and the Lord is with him." At this time he had already slain a lion and a bear, and was soon to slay Goliath. He became Saul's chief minstrel, and his armour-bearer. Clearly, David was no "little child," but was certainly well in his twenties.

We need say no more. It is surely evident that these so-translated "little children" who mocked Elisha were not little children at all, as we understand that expression in English to-day, but were youths and young men whose ages might easily be anything from sixteen to thirty or more; and, since they were a goodly crowd—as is plain from the fact that the forty-two who were mauled by the bears were only a part of the total—probably their ages actually did range between these two figures.

The next thing to note is that these young men who mocked Elisha were of *Bethel*. This is singularly revealing. Bethel was one of the most sacred spots in Israel's land. It was here that Abraham erected his first altar when he came into Canaan (Gen. xii. 8). It was here that young Jacob dreamed his more than a dream, and awoke exclaiming: "Surely the Lord is in this place; and I knew it not!" (Gen. xxviii. 19). It was here in later years that Jacob's name was changed to Israel, following his memorable wrestling with that strange Figure at the brook Jabok (Gen. xxxi. 3). Indeed, Jehovah had named Himself "the God of Bethel" (Gen. xxxi. 13). It was to Bethel, after the nation's settlement in Canaan, that the tribes went up, to consult the Divine Oracle (Judges xx. 18); and Bethel became perhaps the most important centre of Israel's worship of Jehovah (1 Sam. x. 3). In the days of Israel's greatest reformer, Samuel, who founded the "Schools of the Prophets," one of the leading schools of the prophets was planted at Bethel. Yet still later, alas, Bethel suffered a tragic reversal after Solomon's reign, and the disruption of the nation into the northern and southern kingdoms—Israel and Judah. The wicked king Jeroboam erected an idol temple at Bethel, containing a golden calf; and Bethel thenceforth became one of the two main centres of the illicit cultus (1 Kings xii. 28–33). It was against this outrageous perversion of Bethel that Israel's prophets, Hosea and Amos, uttered their invectives, sometime afterwards. For instance, God says through Amos: "In the day that I shall visit the transgressions of Israel upon him, I will also visit the altars of Bethel; and the horns of the altar shall be cut off and fall to the ground" (Amos iii. 14). "The inhabitants of Samaria shall fear because of the calves of Beth-aven (Bethel). . . . Therefore shall a tumult arise

among the people, and all thy fortresses shall be destroyed. . . .
So shall Bethel do unto you because of your great wickedness:
in a morning shall the king of Israel utterly be cut off (Hos.
x. 5–15).

Get the picture, then. Elisha returns from beyond Jordan,
where Elijah has been miraculously swept up to heaven. He
calls, first, at the school of the prophets in Jericho; and then,
after tarrying there several days, goes on to visit the school of
the prophets in Bethel. In Bethel there is this blatant, rival
school of apostasy, a veritable "synagogue of Satan," which
blasphemes the name of Jehovah, and uses every opportunity
to malign Jehovah's prophets who would call the nation back
to the true God. Learning of Elijah's translation, and of Elisha's
coming to Bethel, the young fellows associated with the licentious cult of the golden calf determine to make a public fool of
Jehovah's new leader. The insult which they administer is that
which is recorded in connection with the incident which we are
considering. We begin to see, now, that there is a grimmer
interest in this affair than lies on the surface. These offenders
were not just a crowd of tiny tots uttering their innocent childish
prattle as they saw an elderly man with a hairless pate approach-
ing their town; they were a sullen, insolent band of youths and
young men who chose this way of despising God Himself, by
despising His chosen messenger. Little children would not be
likely either to hit upon so biting a sarcasm or to sally forth in
such a body to insult a prophet. We may suppose that it was
the usual custom for these young fellows of Bethel to jeer at the
Lord's prophets as they went along the streets, calling them by
nick-names, so as to expose them to contempt, and to prejudice
others against them. Indeed, the purpose would be, if possible,
to drive them from the town. When Elisha now appeared at
Bethel, he was actually wearing Elijah's mantle, as the Lord's
chosen prophet-leader; and the public mocking of him was therefore, in a peculiar way, a mocking of God Himself.

The offence of these young men found vocal expression in
the cry: "Go up, thou bald-head! Go up, thou bald-head!"
Now there is far more rudeness and wickedness in these words
than appears at first sight to an English reader. To begin with,

it is far from likely that Elisha was bald. There is not even a hint of it anywhere else; and, besides this, seeing that Elisha lived for fifty years after this incident, he must have been too young, at the time, for ordinary baldness. But whether Elisha was prematurely bald or not, the point is this, strangely enough, that out in the East—even until the present day—the expression "bald-head" is looked on as the very worst term of insult. Used as a word of insult, it has in it, to the easterner, a spite, a slime, a venom, and an implication of despicableness which make it the lowest of insults. You know how, in our own language, there are words which have a quite normal meaning when used in normal ways, but are vile insults when used contemptuously of persons,—such words as "swine" and "bastard." These are rough equivalents of that expression of "bald-head," in the East. When these young men of Bethel flung this epithet at Elisha, they were knowingly using the most vulgar and cutting of insults against one whom they knew to be the prophet of God. If this insult on Elisha, now just appointed to be successor and representative of Elijah, and bearing his prophetic mantle as the chosen prophet of the Lord, had passed unpunished, the idolaters of Bethel would have been hardened in their idolatry, and the cause of God would have been the more damaged.

But their cry to Elisha was *"Go up!"* What did they mean? Had they been at Jericho, their words might have meant "Go up to Bethel," for Bethel was much higher than Jericho, and was reached by an ascending roadway. No such construction, however, can be put upon their words as we hear them uttered at Bethel. When they said "Go up," they were alluding to Elijah's having gone up to heaven, a few days earlier, in a chariot of fire; and they were saying, in effect, to Elisha: "You follow your master! As *he* went up to heaven, so get *you* up too, and away with you!" They would be rid of him, and of all such who disturbed their ways of sin. Thus we see that the offence of these young fellows was very grave. They were of a responsible age. They were the representatives of a wicked movement. Their outrage against Elisha was a public one, and was probably premeditated, and perhaps was one of many such. Their insult was of the rudest kind, and made mock of a Divine miracle. Moreover, their attack on Elisha was, in reality, against Jehovah Himself.

We shall surely not be surprised, therefore, that God intervened to punish. Instead of charging Elisha with spiteful anger in his pronouncing of a curse upon them, we are driven to see that Elisha was but expressing the mind of God concerning them. Had Elisha's word against them been one merely of his own impetuosity, God would not have approved and endorsed it by the miracle of judgment which immediately gave it effect. Elisha spoke not in personal revenge for the indignity done to himself, but as the mouth of the Divine justice, to punish the dishonour done to God.

As for the two bears which came upon these young men, it is well to notice that they mauled only a certain number of them, and that none is said to have been killed. The punishment, however, was far too clearly connected with their blatant folly for them ever to forget it. It may indeed have been that some of them were killed; but as there is no record of this, we think it unlikely.

And who now will dare to say he cannot believe the Bible because it teaches that God sent bears to devour innocent little children, just to satisfy the spite of a man who was riled by their innocent banter? Such critics had better read the old Book a bit more carefully. When the Bible is tested fairly and thoroughly it triumphs every time.

BY WAY OF APPLICATION

And now let us briefly apply this incident in a practical way to ourselves. Mark this man Elisha, as he pauses on that Bethel highway with the godless youths booing him. He stands before us as an illustration of those words which Paul long afterwards wrote to Timothy—*"Yea, and all that will live godly in Christ Jesus shall suffer persecution."* From that day when seraphic Stephen, the protomartyr, fell beneath the stones, crying "Lord, lay not this sin to their charge," the story of the Christian Church has corroborated this Pauline prophecy. Our Lord Himself foresaw what was coming, when He said: "Blessed are ye when men shall revile you, and persecute you, and shall say all manner of evil against you, falsely, for My sake." Maybe, also, Elisha was one of those whom our Lord had in mind when He said: "Rejoice, and be exceeding glad; for great is your reward in heaven: for *so persecuted they the prophets which were before you.*"

Let us settle it in mind that if we are really living godly in Christ Jesus,—if we are living the out-and-out Christian life, we shall be in the world's bad books! A young man came to D. L. Moody and said: "Mr. Moody, I want to be a Christian; but must I give up the world?" Moody characteristically replied: "Young man, if you live the out-and-out Christian life, the *world* will soon give *you* up." If we are popular with the crowd of worldlings, or if we are not penalised in some way for our attachment to Christ, we have good cause to suspect the reality of our Christian life.

We would say to all young Christians: Do not provoke needless hostility; but, on the other hand, do not expect to be popular with the world now that you have become Christ's. Do not shun persecution; and do not fear it when it comes. Be like the early Christians of whom we read: "They departed from the presence of the Council, rejoicing that they were counted worthy to suffer shame for His name."

The world varies its ways of persecuting us. Sometimes it uses the sword, and sometimes the lip of scorn. Most of us can stand the sword far better than derision or sarcasm. Henry Martyn, that prince among missionaries, was exposed both to peril and insult among the Mohammedans in Persia; but he said that he found "sneers were more difficult to bear than brickbats." Let us be ready, and take the world's sneer with cheerful heart; for the Lord is ever at our hand to give grace; and one day He will return in glory to confess us before all men.

But we may apply this Elisha incident in another way; for if on the one hand it reminds us that all who will live godly in Christ Jesus shall suffer persecution, it also warns men that all who live *ungodly*, and persecute God's people, *shall suffer punishment.* Old Testament incidents, as Paul tells us, were recorded for *our* admonition—as warnings and examples to us. Under the old disposition God frequently visited punishment upon persons immediately after their committing of wrongs, so that the connection between the sin and the punishment might be clearly seen. In this present age, the judgment of the ungodly may be deferred; but it is none-the-less certain, and will be awful when at last it falls. Further, if such chastisement was inflicted on those young men who mocked Elisha, what penalties are in store for those who do despite to the Spirit of grace!

This present age is distinctively the age of Divine *grace*, in which a patient God forbears with human sin; but let not boastful worldlings presume. Some years ago the *Witness* related the following incident. George Whale, chairman of the Rationalist Press Association, at a dinner in the "Trocadero," thus spoke slightingly of the Holy Ghost: "The light from some providential spirit or Holy Ghost is said to have guided the Church for some nineteen hundred years. It has not come, and when it does come I venture to suggest it will not have the dazzling effect of the light that fell on the Apostle on his way to Damascus—the light which left him dazzled for the rest of his life."

The two hundred and seventeen guests present greeted his words with appreciative laughter. In a few moments there were only hushed whispers and awe-stricken faces. It was seen that Mr. Whale had collapsed in his chair; and in the instant silence his strangled breathing was the only sound. Doctors rushed to his side, and he was carried from the room, dying. Artificial respiration was at once tried, but death was almost immediate.

The dinner was to have been followed by dancing; and at the moment that Mr. Whale was being carried from the banqueting hall the orchestra in the next room, unaware of the tragic scene from which a screen divided them, could be heard tuning up their instruments. Personally, I do not hesitate to see in that incident a swift Divine rebuke against such a blasphemous mouthing. Let wordy sceptics and daring scorners beware. They may go so far but no farther.

Finally, the young fellows in this Elisha incident mocked at Elijah's *translation* from earth to heaven in the chariot of fire. Even so to-day there are those who mock at the Divinely promised translation of the true Church at the second coming of Christ.

But their light-hearted disdain will yet prove a millstone that will sink them into everlasting shame and contempt. Take heart, fellow-Christian. It must needs be that offences come: but the Lord will succour His own, and will yet descend from heaven. "The Lord Himself shall descend from heaven with a shout, with the voice of the archangel, and with the trump of God. The dead in Christ shall rise first: then we which are alive and remain shall be caught up together with them in the clouds, to meet the Lord in the air. And so shall we ever be with the Lord. Wherefore *comfort one another with these words.*"

> Jesus, my Lord, Thou art coming!
>   The signs are around us to-day.
> Coming, dear Lord, Thou art coming,
>   The times are preparing Thy way.
> Worldwide conditions portentous,
>   Undreamed by our fathers appear;
> Happenings vast and momentous
>   Proclaim that Thy coming is near.
>
> Jesus, my Lord, Thou art coming!
>   Thy spirit assures me within.
> Coming, dear Lord, Thou art coming,
>   To banish the empire of sin.
> Jesus, Thy people are yearning;
>   The race cries unknowing for Thee.
> Oh, for Thy promised returning—
>   Thy face and Thy glory to see!

THE MAN WHO CAME BACK FROM BEYOND

SCRIPTURE SNAPSHOT

Then Jesus therefore said unto them plainly : Lazarus is dead ; and I am glad for your sakes that I was not there, to the intent that ye may believe ; nevertheless, let us go unto him. Thomas therefore, who is called Didymus (Twin), said unto his fellow-disciples, Let us also go, that we may die with Him. So when Jesus came, He found that he had been in the tomb four days already.

.   .   .   .

And Jesus lifted up His eyes, and said : Father, I thank Thee that Thou heardest Me. And I know that Thou hearest Me always : but because of the multitude which standeth around I said it, that they may believe that Thou didst send Me. And when He had thus spoken, He cried with a loud voice : Lazarus, come forth ! He that was dead came forth, bound hand and foot with grave-clothes, and his face was bound about with a napkin. Jesus saith unto them : Loose him, and let him go.

.   .   .   .

Jesus therefore, six days before the Passover, came to Bethany, where Lazarus was, whom Jesus raised from the dead. So they made Him a supper there : and Martha served, but Lazarus was one of them that sat at meat with Him. . . . The common people, therefore, of the Jews learned that He was there : and they came, not for Jesus' sake only, but that they might see Lazarus also, whom He had raised from the dead. But the chief priests took counsel that they might put Lazarus also to death ; because that by reason of him many of the Jews went away and believed on Jesus.—John xi. 14–17, 41–44 ; xii. 1–11 (R.V.).

THE MAN WHO CAME BACK
FROM BEYOND

MANY OF the persons and incidents which move before us in the pages of the New Testament, besides having a real historical value, are so delineated as to become representative of great spiritual truths. The miracles by which our Lord Jesus healed men's bodies are so presented as to illustrate the way in which He heals men's souls. Men like Nicodemus, the secret disciple, and women like Martha, the cumbered server, are so sketched for us that we cannot but perceive them to represent distinctive types of personalities which recur in every generation. It is wonderful how much we may learn from this pictorial kind of teaching. Truths which fail to impress us when we see them merely stated in so many words, stand out and become vivid when we see them in the living characters of persons and incidents which move before us.

Lazarus of Bethany is one such case of this kind of teaching. We are told seven outstanding things about him—seven outstanding facts which together make him a remarkable illustration of regeneration and new life in Christ.

DEAD

First of all, Lazarus is *dead*. In John xi. 14, we read: "Then said Jesus unto them plainly: Lazarus is dead." When the disciples eventually reach Bethany with the Master they find it even so: Lazarus is indeed dead. Martha and Mary each come to Jesus with the lament, "Lord, if Thou hadst been here my brother had not died."

And just as truly as Lazarus was dead physically, so men and women who have not found new life in Jesus Christ are dead *spiritually*. Unconverted friend, will you believe this?— you are spiritually dead. The word of God declares so. Your condition proves you to be so. Away back in Genesis we find God forewarning Adam that if he ate of the forbidden fruit he should die. He said: "In the day that thou eatest thereof thou shalt surely die." This meant something far worse than that Adam should die physically. When Adam disobeyed, he *died to God*. See Adam and his wife hiding from God in that garden. Instead of eagerly drawing near to Him as before, they slink away and crouch behind the shrubs. They had become dead to sympathy with God, dead to love for him, dead to pleasure in Him; and they sought to escape from His presence. You ask for proof that you yourself, apart from Christ, are dead to God? Then test yourself. Do you really *love* God? Do you really *live* for Him? Do you delight to *serve* Him? Do you only desire those things that *please* Him? Do you put God *first* in all your thoughts and plans and doings? Do you love to *pray* to Him? Do you rejoice in the thought of God's moral *governorship* of human life? Or do you push God to the back of your life, or else push Him right out? Would you like to be independent of God's rule? Would you like to get to some corner of the universe where God is not? To be thoroughly honest and frank—Do you wish that there were no God, no accountability to a Supreme Being, and no day of final judgment? If you will answer these questions honestly, you will soon know that you are dead to God—that you are as truly dead spiritually as Lazarus was dead physically.

RAISED

The second fact about Lazarus is that he was *raised*. In chapter xi. 44, we read: "He that was dead came forth." That sleeping clay thrilled to the command of Jesus as He cried with a loud voice: "Lazarus, come forth!" Even the mysterious domain of the grave must obediently bow to the authority of the incarnate Son of God, even as, a little while earlier, the swelling waves of Galilee had meekly subsided into immediate tranquillity at His bidding. Augustine makes the remark that if Jesus had not called forth Lazarus by name, all the dead folk in the vicinity would have come forth at His voice! One day, yet to be, as the Scripture says, all that are in the graves *will* come forth at the voice of the Son of Man—the one class to the resurrection of immortal life, the other class to the resurrection of judgment. But at Bethany, Lazarus is singled out and called alone; and he comes forth. Yes, Lazarus lives again!

And it is nothing less than this that happens in a spiritual sense when a soul is converted to Jesus Christ; for Jesus Christ is the power of God to salvation, to everyone that believeth. As truly as the man in the Gospel story could say: "One thing I know, that whereas I was blind, now I see," so can the soul, regenerated by faith in the risen Saviour, say: "One thing I know, that whereas I was dead, now I live in newness of life through Jesus Christ." In a meeting where Christians were giving testimonies about their conversion, I heard one brother get up and say: "Well friends, I do not know the particular day on which I was born again; but thank God I know well enough that I am *alive!*" Faith in Christ is not any mere mental assent to certain doctrines: it is a simple but deep heart-trust in Him in response to which the Holy Spirit imparts new spiritual life, so that the soul is raised up in "newness of life." Unconverted friend, let it be your first concern to seek this new life in Christ. Oh that you may hear that voice which called forth Lazarus, saying to yourself: "Come forth!"

BOUND

The third thing which we are told about Lazarus is that when he came back from the sepulchre he was *bound*. Verse 44 says: "He that was dead came forth bound hand and foot with graveclothes." I have often tried to picture just how Lazarus reappeared from that dark vault, enfolded with all his funeral attire. Whether he somehow glided out or not it is not easy to know. But the strange fact is there—that he came forth bound. It must have been a sight never to be forgotten by those who beheld it.

And it is equally strange that those of us who have been raised into newness of life in Christ should needlessly remain bound by the graveclothes of our unregenerate days. We allow ourselves to be bound by fear, pride, love of money, love of worldly pleasure, old habits and ways. I know a Christian minister who for years was bound by the smoking habit. He was troubled about it, especially in his times of prayer: yet he could not break free from it. One Sunday he was addressing a large meeting of men. His text was Philippians iv. 13: "I can do all things through Christ which strengtheneth me." Just as he began to read out his text to the men, there struck him, with the impact of a bolt from the blue, the thought: "*You* cannot say that text truthfully about yourself"; and almost before he realised it he found himself saying: "I can do all things through Christ which strengtheneth me—except give up smoking." The men looked amazed; and the preacher himself was amazed that he had allowed himself to speak so. He explained to the men what had happened, and then added: "From this day I will also prove that I can do even *this* thing, through Christ which strengtheneth me." He *did* prove it, and *still* proves it, after years of victory. May our mighty Saviour set each of us free from the graveclothes of our former unregeneracy!

LOOSED

The next thing about Lazarus is that he was *loosed*. In verse 44, Jesus says: "Loose him, and let him go." When the first astonishment at Lazarus's emergence from the tomb had been got over, what loving and eager hands would haste to free him from his sepulchral impediments! Soon he would be freely moving among his loved ones again. Thus Lazarus had now received both life and liberty.

Even so to-day does Jesus free those to whom He gives new spiritual life. He says to all those evil powers and evil desires and evil habits which have bound us: "Loose him, and let him go": and though these evil forces do not loose us with eager hands like those that liberated Lazarus, they are compelled to release their prey; for whereas Jesus merely stood *near* to Lazarus's grave, and brought him forth, He now *indwells* those who believe on Him, and from within He bursts those invisible bonds which bind the soul.

A certain man who had been well-to-do but had fallen lower and lower through slavery to strong drink, was being pleaded with, by a Christian worker, to give up the drink, especially for his suffering wife's sake. The man replied: "Sir, I know the reasonableness of your pleadings, and I loathe myself for drinking as I do; but you just do not understand my plight. When the mad craving comes over me I am so helpless against it that if there were a bottle of whisky on this table, and you were sitting near with a revolver to shoot me if I touched the whisky, I would take it." Yet that man lived to give glad testimony to the fact that Jesus had loosed him from his slavery. A young man came to me in distress about uncontrollable sex passions. He had tried repression, and had sought help in psychology; but his condition had grown worse. Then he came to know the Lord Jesus as his Saviour; and about four months later he came to tell me, with radiant face, that Jesus had "loosed him and let him go." He had found liberation and victory, not through psychology, but in *Christopathy*! Friend, what is it that binds *you*? Is it temper, fear, lying, impure thought or habit, selfishness, jealousy? Whatever it is, our Saviour can loose you and set you free!

FEASTING

Next we see Lazarus *feasting*. In John xii. 1, 2, we read: "Then Jesus, six days before the Passover, came to Bethany, where Lazarus was which had been dead, whom He raised from the dead. There they made Him a supper; and Martha served, but Lazarus was one of them that sat at the table with Him." We have not time here to dwell on the triple type-teaching of this twelfth chapter—Martha representing *service*; and Lazarus representing *communion*; and Mary representing *consecration*. But see the development in the case of Lazarus—dead, raised, bound, loosed, and now feasting!

What joy does this feast of fellowship bring into our lives! It is grand to be "raised" in newness of life, and grander still to be "loosed" from sin's bondage; but it is still more so to find ourselves saying:

> Lord Thou hast made Thyself to me
> A living, bright reality;
> More present to faith's vision keen
> Than any earthly object seen;
> More dear, more intimately nigh,
> Than e'en the closest earthly tie.

WITNESSING

Next we see Lazarus *witnessing*—witnessing to what Christ had done for him. In chapter xii. 9, we read: "Much people of the Jews therefore . . . came not for Jesus' sake only, but that they might see Lazarus also, whom He had raised from the dead." Lazarus was a standing testimony to the power of Jesus. He witnessed by what he *was*. No doubt, too, he witnessed by what he *said*; for many would flock round him, to hear from his own lips some account of the miracle. The Church's Lazaruses are the best apologetic for Christianity—men and women whose character has been transformed by the saving power of the Lord Jesus,— men and women raised from spiritual death, and made "new creatures in Christ Jesus." If such miracles are not happening to-day as numerously as they ought to be, then it is because Christ is not being lifted up before men and women as He ought to be by those who represent Him; for He is still "the power of God unto salvation to everyone that believeth." It is not just heralds or preachers we need if we are to arrest the sceptical out-sider, but *witnesses*—men and women who can affirm out of first-hand experience, the regenerating and emancipating power of Christ.

CONVINCING

Finally, we see Lazarus *convincing* men as to the saving power of the Lord Jesus. In chapter xii. 11, we read: "By reason of him, many of the Jews went away and believed on Jesus." Lazarus was an argument nobody could get over. So are all those men and women to-day whom Christ has raised and loosed and transformed.

The Rev. Samuel Chadwick tells a moving story concerning his early days in the Methodist ministry. As a young Christian minister he saw himself confronted with the problem of bringing the outsider to the house of God. Being inexperienced, he had an inadequate idea of the magnitude and complexity of the task. His confidence lay largely in his own resources. His sermons were prepared with the utmost care; and his energies were given without stint to every form of religious and social activity. Yet little or nothing seemed accomplished, in a vital, spiritual sense.

The minister grew desperate. His resources failed, and he was driven back upon God. A call to united prayer was sounded. In a marvellous way, old sores were healed, and breaches repaired. The Spirit of the Lord fell upon the people in that church, and a real work began.

For weeks the miracle of Christ's raising Lazarus from the dead possessed the preacher. It seemed to set forth just the Divine work they were needing to see done among them. It showed how the people of long ago came to see Lazarus when they would not come to see Jesus Himself, and how, seeing Lazarus alive again, they were brought to believe on Jesus. For weeks that young minister and his little band prayed God to send them a Lazarus—a man so dead and buried in sin that his wickedness had become offensively notorious and hopelessly bad. With unwearying monotony they prayed the Lord to save the worst sinner in the town: *and He did.*

The man came. He was a dreadful character. Everybody knew him. Nobody ever expected he would be any better. So far as the man himself could remember, he had never been to a religious service, except in gaol. He was the terror of the neighbourhood, and did most extraordinary things out of sheer devilry. But he came ; and he came of his own accord ; and he even volunteered to sign the pledge. The band of Christians were eager to pray with him, and get him really converted ; but he said: "Not this time ; one thing at once." A fortnight went by before he came again, and it seemed as though nothing was going to happen after all. Prayer continued unabated, however ; and the answer came. The hearts of the folk in that little chapel nearly stood still as they saw the big, rough fellow, in his working clothes, walk down the aisle, and fling himself on his knees at the communion-rail. That night he became gloriously saved.

Next morning he told all his workmates what had happened. Then, men who before his conversion dared not have spoken a cross word to him persecuted him most cruelly. Yet he stood well,—until one day, as they were blasting, his bar slipped and jammed his finger ; and, before he was aware, an oath escaped him. The men around him laughed derisively ; but their laughter was only for a moment, for he was evidently hurt—in more ways than one. They released his finger, and in compassion wanted to wrap it up. But with the tears on his face—not for the pain of his finger—and with a broken voice, he said: "Nay, I've a bigger wound than this; we'll have that seen to first"; and, surrounded by the men who had heard him swear, he prayed earnestly and with great simplicity for the forgiveness of his sin. Peace came into his soul; and when he got up he said: "It's all right, mates; God has forgiven me. Now we'll have it wrapped up."

The upshot of all this had better be given in Mr. Chadwick's own words. "The news of his conversion spread like wildfire. Hundreds came to church to see the man Christ had raised from the dead. When it was announced that this man would tell the story of his conversion, they flocked from far and near to hear his testimony. We had been trying for months to fill the church, without success; but when this Lazarus stood up to speak of the things of God, it was impossible to get near the place for the crowd. They would not come to hear sermons; they would not come to see Jesus; but they came to see Lazarus, whom Jesus had raised and saved. Hundreds were converted through that one witness. For years he has been a standing proof of God's power. He was an argument that silenced critics. The church was filled, and sinners were saved."

Oh, fellow-Christians, this is the way that revival begins—when such resurrection miracles take place in the house of God, when Lazaruses are raised from the dead, when well-known characters come under the power of the Gospel and are transformed, and when the people outside begin to flock to Christian resorts to make first-hand contacts with what is happening. Let us cry mightily and perseveringly to our God, that such miracles may begin to happen in great number among us again, so that men may come to see Lazaruses, and, by so doing, may be brought to the Lord Jesus Himself. Let us pray for the conversion of "big" sinners, well-known characters whose conversion would mean much by way of public evidence to the saving energy of our Gospel. Lord, give us Lazaruses!—dead! raised! bound! loosed! feasting! witnessing! convincing! A seven-fold miracle! Lord, give us Lazaruses!

THE MAN WHO ROUTED
THE ALIENS

SCRIPTURE SNAPSHOT

And the angel of the Lord came, and sat under the oak which was in Ophrah, that pertained unto Joash the Abi-ezrite : and his son Gideon was beating out wheat in the winepress, to hide it from the Midianites. And the angel of the Lord appeared unto him, and said unto him, The Lord is with thee, thou mighty man of valour. And Gideon said unto him, Oh, my lord, if the Lord be with us, why then is all this befallen us ? and where be all His wondrous works which our fathers told us of, saying, Did not the Lord bring us up from Egypt ? but now the Lord has cast us off, and delivered us into the hand of Midian. And the Lord looked upon him, and said, Go in this thy might, and save Israel from the hand of Midian : have not I sent thee ? And he said unto him, Oh Lord, wherewith shall I save Israel ; behold, my family is the poorest in Manasseh, and I am the least in my father's house. And the Lord said unto him, Surely I will be with thee, and thou shalt smite the Midianites as one man. And he said unto him, If now I have found grace in Thy sight, then shew a sign that it is Thou that talkest with me. . . .

And Gideon saw that he was the angel of the Lord ; and Gideon said, Alas, O Lord God ! forasmuch as I have seen the angel of the Lord face to face. And the Lord said unto him, Peace be unto thee ; fear not : thou shalt not die. Then Gideon built an altar there unto the Lord and called it Jehovah-shalom : unto this day it is yet in Ophrah of the Abiezrites.

And it came to pass the same night, that the Lord said unto him, Take thy father's bullock, even the second bullock of seven years old, and throw down the altar of Baal that thy father hath, and cut down the Asherah that is by it : and build an altar unto the Lord thy God upon the top of this stronghold. . . .

Then the men of the city said unto Joash : Bring out thy son, that he may die ; because he hath broken down the altar of Baal. . . .

But the Spirit of the Lord came upon Gideon ; and he blew a trumpet, and Abiezer was gathered together after him.—Judges vi. 11–34 (R.V.).

THE MAN WHO ROUTED
THE ALIENS

"The Spirit of the Lord came upon Gideon."

—Judges vi. 34.

GIDEON, the fifth judge of Israel, is always counted—and rightly so—as one of the outstanding heroes in Israel's early history. The eleventh chapter of the Epistle to the Hebrews includes him in its classic catalogue of Old Testament worthies who through faith wrought exploits; and I would be the last man to question his right to appear in that illustrious list. Yet if we are rightly to appraise Gideon, we need to realise at the outset that his heroism was not the product of his natural make-up, but the outcome of a transforming spiritual experience through which he passed. It is this which gives Gideon a living significance to ourselves to-day; for the transforming experience through which Gideon passed, *we* may pass through, and with an equally transforming result.

UNCONVERTED GIDEON

When we first see Gideon he cuts a pathetic figure of unbelief. He suddenly appears on the scene in the sixth chapter of the Book of Judges. Verse 11 begins: "And there came an angel of Jehovah and sat under an oak which was in Ophrah, that pertained unto Joash, the Abi-ezrite: and his son Gideon threshed wheat by the winepress, to hide it from the Midianites." Get the mental picture of this furtive-eyed young Hebrew as he nervously threshes out the corn, away from the proper threshing floor, lest some marauding Midianite should pry round and seize the precious food. Like the other young men of his day, he is stricken with fear at the might of Midian. Israel had sinned; and, in consequence, the hand of Midian had prevailed against them. A seven-years' servitude had ensued; and there seemed little enough prospect of

Israel's ever struggling free from the heel of the alien oppressor; for the Midianites had pitilessly exploited the Israelites, and had reduced them to extreme impoverishment. We are told that when Israel had sown, the Midianites and the Amalekites and the children of the east came up as grasshoppers for multitude, and consumed the increase of the earth, leaving no sustenance for Israel, nor for sheep nor ox nor ass: so that Israel was indeed "greatly impoverished." It was under these circumstances that the stealthily-moving Gideon was found secretly threshing the wheat, "by (or rather *in*) the winepress, to hide it from the Midianites." The usual old-time Eastern threshing-floor was an exposed area, prepared and levelled for the purpose, near the field where the wheat was grown: but the *winepress* would be a good distance away, among the vineyards, and was a shallow hollow in the ground, from which the grape-juice ran into a couple of deeper vats. The winepress would little be suspected as being a place where anyone would be flailing grain. Hence the furtive-eyed Gideon's presence there!

Verse 12 continues—"And the angel of the Lord appeared unto him, and said unto him: Jehovah is with thee, thou mighty man of valour!" So, at any rate, reads our English version; but surely the rendering should be, as in the Septuagint Version, "The Lord is with thee, even the Lord mighty in valour"; or "The Lord is with thee, the (not "thou") mighty Man of Valour." It is Jehovah, not Gideon, who is the mighty One of valour!—and the context makes this only too clear. Cast your eye down the context, and note Gideon's reactions to the heavenly visitation.

He gasps out—"Oh, my Lord, if Jehovah be with us, why then is all this befallen us? And where be all His miracles which our fathers told us of, saying, Did not Jehovah bring us up out of Egypt? But now Jehovah hath forsaken us, and delivered us into the hands of the Midianites." This is pretty dismal, is it not?— "Oh! . . . if . . . why? . . . where . . . but . . . "

Verse 14 continues—"And Jehovah looked upon him and said: Go in this thy might, and thou shalt save Israel from the hand of the Midianites: have not *I* sent thee?" These were strong and reassuring words. Gideon's might was to be in the assurance: "Jehovah is with thee," and in the knowledge that Jehovah had said: "Have not *I* sent thee?" But Gideon moans—"Oh, my Lord, wherewith shall *I* save Israel? Behold, my family is poor in Manasseh, and I am the least in my father's house." The Lord replies still further—"Surely I will be with thee; and thou shalt smite the Midianites as one man." Yet even this is not enough for Gideon. He can only stammer out that awkward "if" again— "If now I have found grace in Thy sight, then *show me a sign.*"

There is no doubt about it,—when we first see Gideon he cuts a pathetic figure of unbelief. In that first gasp—Oh!—see the sceptical *surprise* of unbelief. He who should have been expecting Divine intervention could scarce credit it when it came. In the next words—"*If* the Lord be with us," see the *uncertainty* of unbelief. In the next groan—"Why then is all this befallen us?" see the *questioning* of unbelief. In the pathetic sigh—"where be all His miracles?" see the *desolateness* of unbelief. In the words— "But now Jehovah hath forsaken us," see the *complaint* of unbelief. In the words—"Oh, my Lord, wherewith shall *I* save Israel?" see the *false humility* of unbelief. In the next words— "My family is poor in Manasseh, and I am the least in my father's house," see the *resourcelessness* of unbelief. In Gideon's next words—"If now I have found grace in Thy sight," see the *persistent scepticism* of unbelief. In the weak-kneed plea,—"Show me a sign," see the *sign-seeking* of unbelief.

To be sure, in this quick succession of exclamations, lamentations, and bewildered questionings, we have a most enlightening sample of the vocabulary of unbelief. Here are its favourite words—"oh," "if," "why?" "where?" "but," "oh," "wherewith?" "show a sign." We feel as though we need to put our umbrellas up quickly, to keep off the shower of "ohs" and "ifs" and sighs and fears! Let us settle it in our minds—Gideon, unconverted Gideon, was no "Richard of the lion-heart." He was no "mighty man of valour." Unconverted Gideon could no more have lifted up the sword against mighty Midian than a nervous little infant could say "boo" to a goose! We say again that Gideon's heroism was not the product of his natural constitution, but of a revolutionising experience through which he passed.

PARALYSIS THROUGH UNBELIEF

Before we describe that experience, however, we ought to note two things about unconverted Gideon. First, we see in him a sorry example of the *paralysis* which comes through unbelief. A doubt-filled heart gives a nerveless hand and a feeble knee. Before faith in the true God was awakened in the soul of Gideon, he was prostrated by a sense of helplessness and hopelessness. Unbelief ties the hand, and dulls the eye, and shrinks the soul. It is the man of faith who dares and does things. Faith energises: doubt paralyses. Unbelief is self-frustrating. Moreover, *our* unbelief hinders *God's* working for our deliverance and blessing. We are told that even the Lord Jesus could do no "mighty works" at Nazareth, "because of their unbelief." God save us from such unbelief and paralysis! It is that which most curses the Church to-day.

ANALYSIS OF UNBELIEF

Second, in unconverted Gideon we see a patent *analysis* of unbelief. We only need to mark this man's actions and words to see that his unbelief—as is the case with *all* unbelief—arose from, and consisted in, his looking at circumstances instead of looking to God. Gideon's eyes were earth-bound, as his scared expostulations clearly show.

Yes, looking at circumstances instead of looking to God is the certain cause of unbelief. There are two classic instances of this in the Scriptures. See Peter clambering over the side of that rocking vessel, and actually walking on the water to Jesus. As long as he keeps his eye on Jesus he treads the heaving deep; but as soon as he begins to look round at the boisterous billows, his faith collapses, doubts seize him, he begins to sink, and cries out, "Lord, save me!" Turn back to the Book of Numbers. See those twelve men of Israel returning to the camp of Israel after their forty-days' reconnoitring in Canaan. In their report they all agree as to the excellence of the promised land; but ten of them declare that Israel is utterly incapable of occupying it; while the other two—Caleb and Joshua—urge the immediate conquest of it. The difference between the ten and the two was that the ten had their eyes on circumstances, whereas the two had their eyes towards God. The ten unbelieving pessimists put the difficulties between themselves and God, with the result that God looked very small. The two believing optimists put God between themselves and their difficulties, with the result that the difficulties seemed as but the opportunity for God to display His glorious power. Somebody has wittily remarked that these ten men had been outstandingly impressed by four "G's." They saw "Grapes"—that was the first "G." "Great cities"—that was the second "G." "Giants"—that was the third "G"; and they themselves had felt like "Grasshoppers"—that was the fourth "G." Certainly, these ten miserable pessimists *were* grasshoppers: their unbelief had shrivelled them up. On the other hand, Caleb and Joshua, the two men of faith, were big enough to make all those giant sons of Anak quake with fear; for they stood forth before the congregation of Israel, and said, in effect: "Give no heed to these ten men. They have told you of *four* 'G's'; but they have forgotten the fifth and greatest 'G' of all—*GOD!*" Unbelief had completely unsaddled these ten doleful searchers of Canaan, whereas the word of Caleb and Joshua was, "Let us go up at once and possess it; for we are well able to overcome it."

> Faith, mighty faith, the promise sees,
> And looks to that alone;
> Laughs at impossibilities,
> And cries: It shall be done!

It is always the same—looking at circumstances instead of looking to God breeds unbelief; and unbelief begets helplessness. We see this in the sinking Peter. We see it in the ten gloomy spies. We see it in hang-back Gideon.

GIDEON CONVERTED

But look now at Gideon's transforming experience. There were three distinct stages or parts in it; yet the three go together to make up the one vital change.

First of all Gideon became *converted*. We use that word "converted" deliberately here; for it really describes what happened. When the Angel of the Lord at first appeared to Gideon, saying: "The Lord is with thee," Gideon, as we have seen, sceptically replied: "*If* the Lord be with us. . . ." But now, after hearing all that the heavenly Visitor has said, and having seen the miraculous fire breaking out of the rock, to consume the unleavened cakes which had been laid there, Gideon is quite convinced. He forthwith builds an altar to the one true God. See verse 24—"Then Gideon built an altar there unto the Lord, and called it *Jehovah-shalom*." There is a vital significance about that altar. In the Old Testament Scriptures, the altar is ever the place *where God and men meet*. It is the outward symbol of an inward transaction between the human soul and God. When Gideon built that altar to Jehovah, he made a clean break with the past, turned his back upon false gods, and became a worshipper of the one true God. His subsequent behaviour proves this.

Moreover, Gideon gave that significant altar an equally significant *name*. Go back to that twenty-fourth verse—"Then Gideon built an altar there unto the Lord, and called it *Jehovah-shalom*." That word "shalom" is the Hebrew for *peace*—"Jehovah is my peace"! For the first time in his life this young Hebrew came into a sense of peace. And that is always the first thing that happens when we become truly converted to the Lord Jesus—the heart becomes filled with wondrous peace. There is the peace of knowing that all our sins are forgiven by virtue of Christ's atoning death, that we have become reconciled to God, that a living Saviour daily keeps us, and that a heavenly home awaits us in eternity. Oh, my friend, have *you* yet built your altar to the one true God? Nay, I need not ask you if you have *built* such an altar. God Himself has already built it *for* you, on the hill called Calvary. What I ought to ask is: Have you yet *come* to that altar?

> There's a place where life's burdens are lightened,
>   There's a place where the care-worn find rest:
> There's a place where the sad ones are brightened,
>   Where the poor and the needy are blest.

There's a place where life's storm-clouds are parted,
    And the glory of heaven breaks through ;
Where the tear-dimmed and long broken-hearted
    Find strength to begin life anew.

There's a place where life's woundings and scourgings
    Are healed by a heavenly balm ;
There's a place where life's tossings and surgings
    Are stilled into wonderful calm.
There's a place where the shackles are broken,
    Where the prisoners of sin are set free,
Where the word of forgiveness is spoken ;
    And the place is called—CALVARY.

That is the place where a holy, loving God gives us the pardon, peace, power and promise which we need.

Strangely enough, most people seem to think that if they become converted to the Lord Jesus Christ they will *lose* peace and joy, not *find* them. Before my own conversion to Christ I used to have that idea. I thought I would get no peace from religious scruples and from being either teased or definitely resented. I thought, also, that I would lose all joy in life if I had to give up this and that and the other thing, for the sake of being "religious." Little did I then guess the real truth. The first thing that happened when I had really crowned Jesus as my Saviour-King was that my mind was gently flooded with a light and a joy and a peace such as I had never known before. My experience, like that of millions besides, was perfectly in accord with the verse of a little hymn which some of us often sing—

My hardened heart was touched ;
Thy pardoning voice I heard ;
And joy and peace came in,
Through trusting in Thy word.

Oh, that someone whom I now address may hear the Saviour's voice, and come to that altar on Calvary! Believe me, dear friend, if you are filled with unrest about your sin, Calvary is the place to find peace. God has dealt once-for-all with the human sin-problem, on Calvary. There is One who hung on the Cross in your stead, and bore the penalty of your sin. Trust *Him*, and peace will come to you. Trust Him, and then *go on* trusting Him; and you shall know the meaning of Gideon's *Jehovah-shalom*! Your song shall be . . .

> Oh, the peace my Saviour gives! —
> Peace I never knew before;
> And my way has brighter grown,
> Since I learned to trust Him more.

GIDEON CONSECRATED

But now, mark this man again. Not only did he become converted; he became *consecrated*. He offered up himself to the will of God on that altar which he erected; for the altar, besides being the place where a man meets God, is the place where a man *yields* himself to God.

Gideon's consecration to God was tested and proved in a very stirring way. Turn to verses 25–26:

> "And it came to pass the same night, that the Lord said unto him: Take thy father's young bullock, even the second bullock of seven years old, and throw down the altar of Baal that thy father hath, and cut down the grove that is by it: and build an altar unto Jehovah, thy God, upon the top of this rock, in the ordered place; and take the second bullock, and offer a burnt-sacrifice with the wood of the grove which thou shalt cut down."

We only need to think our way back into the circumstances a bit to appreciate what an acute challenge to Gideon's faith and obedience this test was. The command that he should "throw down the altar of Baal" reminds us at once that Gideon lived in a time of widespread religious apostasy. Israel's religious leaders were "Modernists," and had caused the people to err. They had turned away from the good old Gospel of salvation by faith in the God who had brought Israel out of Egypt. They had said:

"How do we know that Jehovah is the only real God, or that He is even the greatest of the gods? After all, we have never seen Him; nor has anybody else ever seen Him. How do we really know that our forefathers were right in what they said about Him? We have only their word for it. They were probably mistaken. Look at the magnificent temples and impressive gods of the surrounding nations. No wonder they despise our own inferior-looking religion. *Their* gods can be *seen*. There can be no doubting their reality. Why should we cling to the worn-out faith of yesterday? Give us modern gods and an up-to-date religion!"

Yes, this was the sort of thing that had been popularised; and Israel had apostatised to the worship of the *Baalim*, or false gods, of the Canaanite peoples. Therefore, for Gideon to desecrate Baal's altar, and erect one to Jehovah in its place, with a sacrifice made upon it, was to run violently counter to the popular will and to invite death. Would Gideon obey?

Well, turn to verse 27: "Then Gideon took ten men of his servants, and did as the Lord had said unto him: and so it was because he feared his father's household, and the men of the city, that he could not do it by day, and he did it by night." Under the circumstances, we will not be disappointed that Gideon did it by night. The point is that *he actually did it.*

And now see the sequel. Beginning at verse 28, we read: "And when the men of the city arose early in the morning, behold the altar of Baal was cast down, and the grove was cut down that was by it, and the second bullock was offered upon the altar that was built! And they said one to another: Who hath done this thing? And when they enquired and asked, they said: Gideon, the son of Joash, hath done this thing. Then the men of the city said unto Joash: Bring out thy son that he may die, because he hath cast down the altar of Baal, and because he hath cut down the grove that was by it."

Things were looking bad for Gideon. But just then a most remarkable surprise came. Look at verse 31. Gideon's white-haired old father stood forth and addressed the angry crowd— "And Joash said unto all that stood against him: Will *ye* plead for Baal? Will *ye* save him? He that will plead for him, let *him* be put to death whilst it is yet morning. If he be a god, *let him plead for himself,* because one hath cast down his altar!" That was a bit of sound commonsense for once. There was no answering it. If Baal could not defend himself, he could not defend anybody else, and he himself was not worth defending.

But the grandest thing about this episode was the unexpected resurrection of *Joash's* faith in the true God. When Gideon took his stand, his father immediately stood with him. Maybe the old man had secretly sighed for the good old days, and had longed that some brave champion of the old-time faith might arise to call his fellow-countrymen back to Jehovah. Now, when his own son unexpectedly stood up for the old-time faith Joash immediately stood by his side.

We may apply this to ourselves. In nine cases out of ten, the reason we have so little influence for Christ among our own kith and kin is that we ourselves are not prepared to go the length of full obedience to God's will for us. We give way in this and that and the other thing, to make our Christianity more compatible with the usual standards. If we were fully obedient to our Lord's will, perhaps our loved ones would be won for the Saviour in surprising ways.

> We fail to win another's heart
>   Because of failure in our own;
> We strive to play a vital part,
>   Yet sink, self-foiled, and weep alone.
> Ah, were we set to do *God's* will,
>   How different would the story be!
> What purpose high would life fulfil,
>   With meanings for eternity!

GIDEON CONTROLLED

Finally, Gideon became *controlled,* by which we mean that he became controlled by the Spirit of God. See verse 34—"But the Spirit of the Lord came upon Gideon: and he blew a trumpet; and Abi-ezer was gathered after him." This man, who was first *converted* to the true God, then *consecrated* to the will of God, and then *controlled* by the Spirit of God, became at once a leader and a saviour of his people. The people recognised the trans-forming power of God within him, and flocked to him when he sounded his clarion. The story which follows, in the Scripture account, tells of Gideon's marvellous victory over Midian, and the freeing of Israel from the alien yoke.

What a transformation had now taken place in Gideon! The most transforming thing of all was his becoming controlled by the Holy Spirit. Mark well that thirty-fourth verse, which says that "the Spirit of the Lord came upon Gideon." The construc-tion here, in the Hebrew, is remarkable. A near translation would be: "The Spirit of Jehovah *clothed Himself* with Gideon" —as with a garment. The Hebrew word means to *put on* so as to *fill*. This, then, was the man God used—*converted, consecrated, controlled*.

What a sermon, then, is this man to us! Like Abel, "he being dead, yet speaketh." This soul-saving, life-changing, character-transforming experience through which he passed may be known by ourselves to-day—not, of course, in its outward accidentals, but in its inward essentials. *We* may be truly converted to God, consecrated to His will, and controlled by His Spirit. The Holy Spirit, who at Pentecost became Christ's abiding provision for all His people throughout this present dispensation, may clothe Himself with our own personalities just as truly as He clothed Himself with Gideon,—clothe Himself with us so as to make our lives holy and our character Christlike, so as to keep us sweet and gracious and constant amid trying circumstances, so as to change our dismal defeat into exploits of victory, and so as to equip us with spiritual power for effective Christian service. Yes, *we* may know this experience.

We must clearly understand, however, that there can be no experiencing of the Holy Spirit's infilling until we have become truly converted and consecrated. We must come to Calvary's altar. We must see the holy Son of God dying for our sins. We must take pardon from that pierced hand, and become reconciled to God "through the death of His Son." Then we must offer ourselves as "living sacrifices" to God, so that we may "prove what is that good and acceptable and perfect will of God" for us. When God's Spirit has thus claimed *us*, we, on our part, may reverently but confidently claim *Him*; and He will not fail us. This experience may really be ours. Let us not look to circumstances, or faith will begin to fail. We must keep our eye on the promise of God. Look up those wonderful verses in the New Testament which speak about being filled and controlled and led and used by the Holy Spirit; and then, if you are really yielded up to Christ, claim their fulfilment in your own life. Let faith in the word of God tread down the sneaking doubts which come through looking at circumstances. Really yield to Christ, and really trust Him. Then you will certainly find that Frances Ridley Havergal's words are right—"They who trust Him wholly, find Him wholly true."

> Doubt sees the obstacles ;
>   Faith sees the way
> Doubt sees the darksome night ;
>   Faith sees the day.
> Doubt dreads to take the step ;
>   Faith soars on high.
> Doubt whispers: "Who believes?"
>   Faith answers—"I!"

THE MAN WHO WAS REBUKED
BY HIS ASS

And Balak the son of Zippor was king of Moab at that time. And he sent messengers unto Balaam the son of Beor, to Pethor, which is by the River, to the land of the children of his people, to call him, saying, Behold there is a people come out from Egypt : behold, they cover the face of the earth, and they abide over against me : come now therefore, I pray thee, curse me this people ; for they are too mighty for me : peradventure I shall prevail, that we may smite them, and that I may drive them out of the land : for I know that he whom thou blessest is blessed, and he whom thou cursest is cursed. . . . And God said unto Balaam : Thou shalt not go with them ; thou shalt not curse the people ; for they are blessed. . . .

And Balak sent yet again princes, more, and more honourable than they. And they came to Balaam, and said unto him : Thus saith Balak, the son of Zippor, Let nothing, I pray thee, hinder thee from coming unto me ; for I will promote thee unto very great honour. . . .

And Balaam rose up in the morning, and saddled his ass, and went with the princes of Moab. And God's anger was kindled because he went ; and the angel of the Lord placed himself in the way for an adversary against him. Now he was riding upon his ass, and his two servants were with him. And the ass saw the angel of the Lord standing in the way, with his sword drawn in his hand ; and the ass turned aside out of the way, and went into the field : and Balaam smote the ass, to turn her into the way. . . .

So Balaam went with the princes of Moab.

.   .   .   .

How shall I curse whom God hath not cursed ?
And how defy whom Jehovah hath not defied ?
Who can count the dust of Jacob ?
Or number the fourth part of Israel ?
Let me die the death of the righteous,
And let my last end be like his !

—Numbers xxii, 5–35, xxiii, 8–10 (R.V.)

THE MAN WHO WAS REBUKED
BY HIS ASS

OUR subject is that strange personage, the hireling prophet, Balaam. He figures in Numbers xxii.–xxiv. The three chapters, which are a complete section in themselves, are notable for their literary form and style. It has been well observed that the skill with which the complex character of this wizard prophet is drawn, the felicity with which he is contrasted with the crude simplicity of king Balak, the picturesque grandeur of scenery and incident, and the art with which the drama-like story leads up by successive stages to the final triumph of God and Israel, are worthy, from an artistic viewpoint, of the greatest of the dramatic poets.

The three chapters are a parenthetic episode, giving a glimpse of what was going on in the camp of Israel's enemies. Israel, a vast host of some two million, had been brought out of Egypt by a mighty intervention of Jehovah, had been given the Law at Sinai, had been organised into orderly mobility, and had travelled with twenty halts in eleven months, the two hundred miles from Sinai to Kadesh-barnea on the border of the promised land. Then, at the Kadesh-barnea crisis, they had succumbed to the pessimism of the ten spies, faith had failed, morale had snapped, mutiny had flared out, organization had temporarily collapsed, and the people had been consigned to the thirty-eight years' "Wandering," during which they had pasturised and shepherded in the open country of Paran and Zin.

But now the long delay was over. The pillar of cloud and fire had lifted from the Tabernacle again. The people were to march once more. They had ceased to be roving nomads, and had become God's pilgrims again with a settled objective. In about four months they move from the Kadesh vicinity to the Plains of Moab, east of Jordan, opposite Jericho. On route they register victory after victory. One after another the giant cities of Bashan go down before them: and now they face Moab. The two kingdoms, Moab and Midian, are blanched with fear. What are they to do?

This is where Balaam comes in. The Moabites, "willing to wound, but fearing to strike," felt it vain to fight while Israel manifestly enjoyed the blessing of a God seemingly mightier than Moab's gods; but they thought it might be possible to neutralise that advantage by laying on them the heavy ban of some counteracting magical power. For this purpose the prophet Balaam was urgently invited.

Such a notion may seem queer to us to-day, yet it was simply a distorted survival of the fact that generations earlier the true God had indeed communicated not infrequently with men. So king Balak sends for Balaam, away up on the Euphrates, eighteen days' distance or so from Moab. Balak apparently knew that Balaam was a prophet of the supreme God, and he realized that to get such a prophet to put a curse on Israel would do what all the fighting forces of Moab and Midian could not do. What a sinister thing this, to send for one to invoke the curse of the supreme Power upon a nation! One thing stands out strikingly, however, which it is well to note: the Moabites, in sending for the famous Balaam, did at least reveal a keen sense of the truth that a spiritual power can only be matched by a spiritual weapon —and that is more than can be claimed for millions of our well-educated, gross-minded moderns! What is more, this sensing of the truth that a spiritual problem can only be matched by a spiritual power seems strangely lacking on the part of *church leaders* to-day. The real power of the Church lies not in the pockets of the rich men associated with it, not in the social prestige of its personnel, not in the intellectuality of its representatives, not in outward amalgamations, but in the supernatural empowerment of Pentecost. We have allowed natural wisdom to supplant spiritual vision. We have substituted clever method for wrestling in prayer. We have wanted to make an outward show, and have lost inward dynamic.

But we are branching out too soon! For the moment, we must stick closely to the Balaam drama itself. Let us see what happens when Balaam is sent for. The first embassy to him is reported in chapter xxii. 1–14 (which please read again). With it we get our first surprise: we find that Balaam is a prophet of *Jehovah*! Note verse 8, "He said unto them: Lodge here this night, and I will bring you word again, as Jehovah shall speak unto me." How did this eastern soothsayer know the true God, and how could he have such dealings with Him?

THE DOUBLE-MINDEDNESS OF BALAAM

Before we linger over this problem, let us get the fuller portrait of the man. Follow the developing revelation of his *double-mindedness*. Plainly Balaam knew that the people whom he was being asked to curse were the objects of Jehovah's special favour. See verse 12, "Thou shalt not curse the people, for they are blessed. Therefore, a decisive refusal was the only course for a true prophet, and Balaam knew it. Yet see how he behaved. He knew he should not accompany these men, and feared to incur the Divine displeasure; yet the "rewards of divination" were there, in their hands before him (verse 7), and these acted strongly on his covetous mind. Between the two influences he parleyed with temptation. What he did was to obey God in outward semblance yet convey to the Moabite princes that his own real desire was to go with them. See how he puts it to them: "Jehovah refuseth to give me leave to go with you." The hint was that he himself wished to go; and this is just how the Moabite delegation took it, as the later verses show. He would have run greedily for the reward, and was only restrained by a servile fear of God. Had he flatly refused, he would have been saved further temptations; but the impression conveyed to Moab was that further inducements might prevail upon him, and so a new embassage was dispatched to him, with more handsome bribes (see verses 15–17).

Balaam's answer to this second appeal was worthy of any prophet, if only it had expressed what was deepest in his heart: "If Balak would give me his house full of silver and gold, I cannot go beyond the word of Jehovah my God, to do less or more" (18). Well spoken, Balaam! Then why not at once dismiss the Moabite deputation? But no, instead, Balaam betrays the irresoluteness which always characterises a double-minded man: "Now therefore I pray you, tarry ye here this night also, that I may know what Jehovah will say to me more" (19). God knew well enough what was in this man's mind, and, as is always so in such circumstances, while He sought to deter Balaam from folly and sin, He would not violate the human power of *choice*. So God now allows Balaam to go, but He puts an interdict on his lips (for while God allows human freewill wide limits, He will not allow it to thwart His own sovereignty). Verse 20 says: "And God came to Balaam at night and said unto him: If the men be come to call thee, rise up, go with them, but only the word which I speak unto thee, that shalt thou do." Balaam is pleased. Apparently he has gained a point. Verse 21 says, "And Balaam rose up in the morning, and saddled his ass, and went with the princes of Moab."

And what then? Verse 22 says, "And God's anger was kindled because he went; and the angel of Jehovah placed himself in the way for an adversary against him." But *why* was God angry if he had given him permission? It was because God knew that although He had forbidden Balaam to curse Israel, Balaam's secret intent *was* to curse Israel for the sake of the carnal reward. Yet although angry, it was in mercy that God now sought to obstruct Balaam's going; and it was in this connection that there occurred the strange Divine intervention in which Balaam was rebuked by his ass. See verses 21–35.

Do we need spend any time arguing the *credibility* of this strange miracle? Those of us who accept Genesis i. 1, "In the beginning, God created the heaven and the earth," will have no difficulty in accepting the physical possibility of *this* little miracle. And as for its *probability*, who is that wonderfully wise man who will determine for us just in what ways almighty God may or may not have thought it wise or needful to intervene at different times? The fact is that this ass incident, like all other supernatural occurrences recorded in the Scriptures, stands or falls simply according to our answer to the one, vital, all-comprehending question, "Is the Bible the inspired word of God?" If we answer "Yes" to that question, we shall have no fundamental difficulty in accepting *any* of its parts, including this Balaam episode. The Bible certainly *claims* right through to be the word of God (and in no part more definitely than in the Pentateuch, where the Balaam chapters occur). To ourselves, there are thoroughly scientific reasons for accepting it as such, and therefore we have no difficulty in accepting this strange abnormality that Balaam's ass was suddenly caused to speak with human voice and language.

The *significance* of the incident, of course, is that God Himself was speaking to the disobedient prophet by exceptional means in order to save him from his own stupid folly. Balaam, however, persisted, and eventually reached Moab, secretly indulging the idea that somehow he might manage to "wangle" the desired curse on Israel, and then receive the alluring rewards of king Balak. But "God is not mocked." Balaam was simply fooling himself. He was in for a double frustration—for he was made to bless the people he had come to curse, and instead of gaining Balak's rewards he incurred his bitter anger!

THE PROPHECIES OF BALAAM

Three times Balaam now approaches Jehovah on behalf of Balak against Israel. See chapter xxiii. Before each approach seven altars are built, seven bullocks and seven rams are offered. But each time Balaam is made to bless the flock he fain would have cursed, until the exasperated Balak exclaims, "I called thee to curse mine enemies, and, behold, thou hast altogether blessed them these three times! Therefore now flee thou to thy place! I thought to promote thee unto great honour; but lo, Jehovah hath kept thee back from honour!" After the first approach, Balaam is sent back to Balak with the following message:

> From Aram hath Balak brought me,
> Moab's king, from the mountains of the East:
> > Come, curse me Jacob,
> > And come, defy Israel.
> How shall I curse whom God hath not cursed?
> And how defy whom Jehovah hath not defied?
> For from the top of the rocks I see him,
> And from the hills I behold him—

> Lo, it is a people that dwell alone,
> And shall not be reckoned among the nations.
> Who can count the dust of Jacob,
> Or number the fourth part of Israel?
> Let me die the death of the righteous,
> And let my last end be like his!

Such words were far from comforting to Balak; and the message after the *second* approach (18–24) was decidedly disconcerting. The climax was reached in the message after the *third* approach (xxiv.), ending with these words concerning Israel:

> Blessed be every one that blesseth thee
> And cursed be every one that curseth thee.

Nor is this all. In an inspired addendum, Balaam breaks forth:

> There shall come forth a star out of Jacob,
> And a sceptre shall rise out of Israel,
> And shall smite through the corners of Moab,
> And break down all the sons of tumult;
> And Edom shall be a possession,
> Even Seir, his enemies, a possession;
> While Israel shall do valiantly,
> And out of Jacob shall one have dominion.

At the end of this final prophecy we read: "And Balaam rose up, and went and returned to his place; and Balak also went his way." The chapter adds no more; yet there is a sorry sequel to Balaam's visit, in connection with which we learn that between these prophesyings and his departure, he gave Balak certain subtle and immoral advice which nearly ruined Israel. Oh, the strange, despicable meanness of this prophet-hypocrite! While in a real way a prophet of Jehovah, he is reprobate at heart. For the sake of base, personal gain, he would gladly have used his prophetic prerogative to curse the very chosen of Jehovah, had he been permitted. And even when he knew the special care and favour of Jehovah toward Israel, he whispered a filthy suggestion to Balak with a view to seducing Israel's son by means of the Moabite and Midianite women! Balaam is the Judas of the Old Testament prophets.

THE THREE PROBLEM FEATURES OF BALAAM

We have now got the full portrait of this strange personage, and we find three problematical features presenting themselves to us—(1) his knowledge of the true God, (2) his enigmatical character, (3) his strange prophetic gift.

First, then, how shall we account for Balaam's *knowledge of the true God*? We believe he is one of the many evidences of an original, pure revelation of God which became obscured and perverted as time elapsed and the human race dispersed throughout the earth. Balaam was of Pethor (Num. xxii. 5), and Pethor was in Mesopotamia (Deut. xxiii. 4); so that he came from the very cradle of the race; and the natural explanation of his knowledge of the true God is that such knowledge had far from disappeared at that time from that region. The descendants of Nahor in their Mesopotamian home were substantially one with the chosen family of Abraham in religious beliefs. Bethuel and Laban acknowledged the same God as Isaac and Jacob (Gen. xxiv., xxxi.). Generations had passed since then, and probably many idolatrous practices had developed among the common people; yet the lapse of time makes little difference to the secret and higher teaching of countries like the Mesopotamia of that age. Men like Balaam, who probably had an hereditary claim to his position as seer, remained purely monotheistic in creed, and in their hearts called only on the God of Abraham and Nahor, the true God.

Second, what about Balaam's *enigmatical character*? He is a walking paradox, a true prophet and a false both in one. He is a true prophet in that he knows the true God, has real communications with Him, and transmits real messages from Him; yet he is a false prophet in that he also resorts to magical arts and prostitutes his prophetic gift for base gain. How shall we explain such an unhallowed blend? A commentator aptly says: "This is undeniably one of the instances in which the more trained and educated intelligence of modern days has a distinct advantage over the simpler faith of the first ages. The compromise in Balaam between true religion and superstitious imposture, between an actual divine inspiration and the practice of heathen sorceries, between devotion to God and devotion to money, was an unintelligible puzzle to men of old. But to those who have grasped the character of a Louis XI, or an Oliver Cromwell (and shall we add, a Hitler?), or have gauged the mixture of highest and lowest in some of the religious movements of modern history, the wonder is not that such an one should have been, but that such an one should have been so simply yet so skilfully depicted."

Third, what of Balaam's *prophecies*? We believe that although his other recorded sayings and doings were far from inspired, his Israel prophecies were really inspired utterances. See chapter xxiii. 5, 16. In chapter xxiv. 2, we are clearly told that "the Spirit of God came upon him." But how could the Holy Spirit come upon such an one as this double-minded Balaam? He came upon him, not because Balaam was a worthy vehicle, but despite him, crushing his secret thought to curse Israel, and overriding the stratagems of hypocrisy, so that he who would fain have cursed Israel for reward was *compelled* to be the mouthpiece of marvellous benedictions. Eventually, Balaam himself was driven to realize this, and ceased further use of "enchantments" (xxiv. 1).

PRACTICAL LESSONS FROM BALAAM

With the full figure of this Jekyll-and-Hyde prophet now in view, let us draw certain practical lessons. First of all, Balaam is a red lamp of warning to all of us who hold sacred office in the Christian ministry or in religious organisations. He shows us that *it is dangerously easy to hold a spiritual office with a carnal motive.* We do well to watch against this ever-present peril with unrelaxing vigil, for Balaam is by no means a solitary victim of it. He had more than a few companions in Old Testament times, and he has all too many successors in modern days. Oh, let those of us who bear the ark of God beware! Let the sons of Levi, and those who don the mantle of the prophet take heed! If Satan cannot pervert our theology he will try to get our eyes fixed on fees and emoluments and self-advancement. If he cannot vitiate our message he will try to vitiate our motive. I know this is delicate ground; ministers and evangelists can be treated so shabbily by thoughtless church office-bearers and short-sighted committees; yet the warning is seasonable.

Second, Balaam is a danger-signal to all of us in the matter of a strange yet all-too-real form of hypocrisy. *It is possible to be spiritual without being moral.* The chairman of a local "Keswick" once made a remark which I cannot forget: "It is possible to be moral without being spiritual; and it is possible to be spiritual without being moral." Most of us understand how true the first part of that comment is, for we know people who live morally upright lives yet have never been "born again" spiritually; but the real sting of that chairman's remark is in its tail—that it is possible to be "spiritual without being moral." Alas, it seems true, however strange. Balaam is not the only such enigma. We have met convention-going Christian persons who could talk on the deeper experiences of sanctification with spiritual-sounding phraseology and seemingly sympathetic spiritual insight, who nevertheless could condescend to grovelling behaviour and tricks of meanness which the average man in the street would blush to own. Beware! There is a subtle, gradual, unintentional kind of hypocrisy into which it is easy for any of us to backslide by an almost imperceptible downgrade. Having become known as Christian believers, it is easy to slip into merely maintaining an outward profession when there is inward breakdown of prayer and Bible-meditation and fellowship with Christ. We feel discomfort about this at first, but if it is not checked it gradually produces a callous state in which our "Christian life" so-called is nothing but an habitual professionalism. We have not *meant* to be hypocrites, but we *are*: and from that point it is only a step further to *deliberate* hypocrisy.

But again, Balaam shows us that *to know the will of God and yet put selfish interests first is a form of madness.* Peter says, "The dumb ass, speaking with man's voice, forbad the *madness* of the prophet" (2 Pet. ii. 16). How many of us would do well to heed this lesson! Especially does it need bringing home to our younger men and women as they choose careers and plan for the future. What sad illustrations could be given! How many there are who, although they have known the will of God to be otherwise, have chosen careers of their own determining, or have become linked in wedlock with partners whom God never intended for them, only to find in painful experience later that it is indeed a costly folly knowingly to choose other than the will of God!

And again, Balaam shows us that *amid great privileges it is possible to miss God's highest and best.* Unreal as Balaam's "divinations" were, he had real communications from the true God which might have made him a diffuser of spiritual illumination to his fellows. But he did not genuinely respond to the call of the highest. His name might have become one of the alpha stars of history, but he did not rise to his opportunities and turn his privileges to the glory of God. He missed the highest, and deteriorated to the lowest.

Further, in Balaam we see *the folly of trusting to fleeting desires after a better life.* Listen to his pious exclamation in chapter xxiii. 10: "Let me die the death of the righteous, and let my last end be like his!" Yes, he meant it, this queer mixture of a man, but his fascinatedness with the temporary gratifications of this present world made his desires after spiritual things spasmodic. He wished to die the death of the righteous, but was not disposed to live the *life* of the righteous. Hence, his sentimental wish was as futile as the mirage of the desert. Balaam has no lack of posterity. Thousands desire the rewards of godliness, which they cannot but admire, yet they never really yield themselves to God and submit to the healthful *discipline* of godliness. Most people, even the worst, have desires after a better life, from time to time, but unless these are resolutely acted upon they are worse than useless. They but increase our guilt without remedying our condition. I know people who are moved to tears by touching anecdotes in sermons, and who again and again are excited to a realization of their need of Christ, who nevertheless allow these periodic longings and awakenings to come to nothing because they somehow cannot tear their minds from the mesmerism of earthly things. They are often *going* to become Christians, yet they never *do.* Their hell will be all the darker in the end.

But once more, in Balaam we see *the utter depths to which men are brought by the systematic resistance of conscience.* The most dastardly thing about Balaam is that which we now mention. He knew that his intended cursing of Israel had been divinely turned into blessing; yet before he left Balak he gave him certain unclean advice with a view to ruining by sexual seduction the people whom Jehovah purposed to bless! (See chapter xxv.) In chapter xxxi. 16 we read: "Behold, these caused the children of Israel to commit trespass *through the counsel of Balaam.*" Yes, this detestable Balaam was the evil genius behind this revolting trickery.

Let all of us beware. Those who systematically resist conscience are their own biggest enemies. They are forging the chains of their own damnation. Bit by bit conscience ceases to function properly, until, despite a head knowledge of religion, evil tempers dominate the heart, and debase the moral sense to depths which at one time would have seemed unthinkable. What a fool this Balaam was!—he had enough religious conviction to restrain him outwardly but not enough to direct him inwardly; he was afraid to go too far outwardly lest God should punish him, but he inwardly *wanted* to, that Balak might reward him; so he played about with conscience and resorted to hypocrisy and self-deception. But did he benefit? He missed the rewards of *this* world because he was obliged to remain outwardly conscientious, and he missed the rewards of the *next* world because he was inwardly corrupt. In the Scriptures there are characters far more blatantly wicked than Balaam, yet from cover to cover is there a more despicable figure than this double-minded prophet-hypocrite?

THE THREEFOLD NEW TESTAMENT COMMENT

Perhaps before we leave Balaam, we ought just to note the three New Testament references to him. In 2 Peter ii. 15 we read of "the *way* of Balaam." In Jude verse 11 we read of "the *error* of Balaam." In Revelation ii. 14 we read of "the *doctrine* of Balaam." Three evils—"the way . . . the error . . . the doctrine" of Balaam. What are they? The "*way*" of Balaam is the prostitution of a spiritual gift for selfish gain. The "*error*" of Balaam is the idea that the will of God may be circumvented under cover of an outward respect for His Name. The *"doctrine"* of Balaam is the counsel to ruin by fleshly seduction the people who cannot be cursed by Divine permission.

Thus clearly the New Testament has this pretender "sized up" —which is only another way of saying that *God* saw right through him; and the New Testament comments reveal God's judgment on him.

Finally, to end on a very different and much brighter aspect of this Balaam episode, see *the triumph of God and Israel despite all the stratagems of evil.* Look down from the mountains of Moab to the plain stretching away below. See there the tents of Israel, stretching away in their thousands. It is a peaceful scene. Little did the children of Israel think that so near to them there was actually a prophet of Jehovah from the banks of the Euphrates, seeking by all the contrivances of divination to bring the divine curse upon them. But see how God overrules the devices of evil, for the furtherance of His own sovereign purposes and the final blessing of the elect people. The Spirit of inspiration comes upon Balaam, as desired, but in a way which makes the man defeat his own intention, and causes him to become the mouthpiece of Jehovah to inform heathen nations of the ultimate purpose through Israel.

> There shall come forth a star out of Jacob,
> And a sceptre shall rise out of Israel. . . .

Look at Israel again, down there in that valley, and be reminded of Isaiah's words: "No weapon that is formed against thee shall prosper." That has been true from Balaam's day to Adolf Hitler's. Very soon now, if we mistake not the signs of the times, we shall see the culminating demonstration of this truth, and immediately thereupon the "Star" will flash forth from Jacob, and the "Sceptre" will rise out of Israel, for Christ shall reappear in the splendour of His second advent. He shall take the throne of David. Invention shall be no more prostituted to the furtherance of war and wickedness. Science and art shall pay tribute at His feet. War shall be banished. All nations shall be comprehended in His millennial empire. "Even so, Lord Jesus, come quickly!"

THE MAN WHO WENT AWAY
GRIEVED

SCRIPTURE SNAPSHOT

And as He was going forth into the way, there ran one to Him, and kneeled to Him, and asked Him, Good Master, what shall I do that I may inherit eternal life ? And Jesus said unto him, Why callest thou me good ? none is good save one, even God. Thou knowest the commandments, Do not kill, Do not commit adultery, Do not steal, Do not bear false witness, Do not defraud, Honour thy father and mother. And he said unto him, Master, all these things have I observed from my youth. And Jesus looking upon him loved him, and said unto him, One thing thou lackest : go, sell whatsoever thou hast, and give to the poor, and thou shalt have treasure in heaven : and come, take up the cross and follow me. But his countenance fell at the saying, and he went away sorrowful : for he was one that had great possessions.—Mark x. 17–22 (R.V.).

THE MAN WHO WENT AWAY GRIEVED

"When Jesus was gone forth into the way, there came one running, and kneeled to Him, and asked Him: Good Master, what shall I do that I may inherit eternal life? . . . And he went away grieved; for he had great possessions."—Mark x. 17–22.

WE ARE not surprised that Matthew, Mark and Luke all record this incident, for it touches a sensitive chord in most human hearts. Those who witnessed the interview between this superior-looking young aristocrat and the peasant Prophet of Galilee would never forget it. Such incidents stamp themselves on the mind with ineffaceable permanence.

And what shall we say about this rich young ruler? Never did a young man display brighter promise. Never did a young man break down more pathetically. On the one hand we cannot but sing his praises. On the other hand we cannot but mourn his failure.

HIS LAUDABLE QUALITIES

First, then, let us sing his praises as we think of his laudable qualities.

See his *eagerness*. Mark tells us that he came "running" to Jesus. He has heard the teaching of Jesus, and has watched Jesus Himself. His mind is made up. He must get to Jesus. He is too eager to delay, especially so since Jesus has now "gone forth into the way," and is about to leave this district of Peræa, on His way up to Jerusalem. No time shall be lost. There shall be no postponement. So with eager haste, he now comes "running" to Jesus.

How admirable is such eagerness toward Christ! Would that there were more of it to-day! The greatest thing we can ever do is to come to the Lord Jesus; for He alone can save our souls. Yet what foolish hanging back there is by many who know far more about the Saviour than did this rich young ruler who came "running" to Him! Let us note well, then, this young man's eagerness.

Next see his *humility*. He not only came running; he *"kneeled"* before Jesus. This, of course, was not an act of worship; but it was an expression of utmost respect, perhaps even of veneration. When we consider the social difference between this rich young ruler and Jesus, we cannot but be impressed by the beautiful humility which this act of kneeling exhibits. He was rich, probably very rich, for he had "great possessions." Then he was a "ruler," as Luke tells us, which probably means that he was a ruler in the synagogue, or possibly a member of the highest council in the land. He was one of the magistrates; perhaps the youngest J.P. on the Bench. Both by possession and position he was in the highest rank of society. His style and quality of dress, not to mention his personal appearance and bearing, would indicate his social superiority. Furthermore, that he should be already a "ruler" while comparatively young strongly suggests that he was a young man of outstanding gifts, of recognised integrity, and of exceptional promise.

Behold this elegant young man of culture hasting to the plainly-clad peasant Prophet of Galilee and kneeling before Him to ask for spiritual guidance. Can you not see it vividly with the eye of your imagination? This young man's aristocratic connections seem to have increased rather than impaired his courtesy and humility.

I wish there were more humility before Christ, and more reverence toward the things of God, among the youth of to-day. We are much behind our parents in that respect. Modern youth may have many fine qualities; but it is deficient in its capacity for reverence—much to its own discredit and loss. We may learn much from the humility of this young ruler.

But now observe this young man's *courage*. Despite his high social standing he made no attempt to conceal his sense of need and his admiration for Jesus, as many others did. He did not seek for a private interview, or come by night, as Nicodemus did. He came to Jesus in broad daylight, on the main road, and in the presence of all. Yes, although the Scribes and Pharisees and most of his own social class were openly despising Jesus, this high-born young man came to Jesus and even did obeisance at His feet in that public way.

What commendable courage he thus shows us! To all who would fain come to Jesus but hold back through the fear of man, the example of this fine young fellow says: "Have the courage of your convictions. Come out into the open, and confess your allegiance to the Saviour!"

See also this rich young ruler's *discernment*. He comes to Jesus saying *"Good Master."* He knew true worth and goodness where he saw it. No disparity of social position between himself and Jesus could prevent him from perceiving in Jesus a unique manifestation of heavenly wisdom. Like Nicodemus, this young man saw in Jesus "a teacher sent from God." Indeed, his use of that expression *"Good* Master" may indicate that he discerned the moral sublimity of Jesus even more truly than did many who were professed disciples; for our Lord took hold of that word "good," in His reply: "Why callest thou Me good? there is none good but One, that is God." It need scarcely be said that in these words our Lord was far from disclaiming His own deity. He was saying, in effect, "Believing Me to be merely a human teacher, as you do, why do you apply to me a term which in reality belongs to God alone?" Or is there really a deeper significance here, namely, that this rich young ruler had discerned in Jesus something more than the merely human, and was addressing Him as "Good Teacher" with a thoughtfulness which was more than mere courtesy? I incline to think so. But without staying to discuss that, let me ask: Have we ourselves discerned this divine goodness in Jesus? Have *we* seen in Him the one really "good" Teacher of men, and the only Saviour of sinners? It is the first step toward eternal life when we see Him as such.

Still further, see this rich young ruler's *spirituality*. He comes to Jesus with the solemn, urgent, vital question: "What must I do to inherit *eternal life?*" He has a mind for spiritual and heavenly things. He comes not to have his body healed of some malady, or to plead for the cure of someone in his household, but to enquire about the salvation of his *soul*. No man ever came on a better errand than that. Most men enquire for the good to be obtained in this present world; but this rich young ruler was concerned about the life to come. He was no Sadducee, doubting this and that and the other thing in the name of so-called "reason." He believed in the reality of spiritual things. Though he was young, he felt he ought not to procrastinate. Though he was rich he did not disdain to confess such spiritual concern. Though he was a leader in the synagogue, he did not conceal the fact that despite his profession of religion he was nevertheless still longing and really anxious to find the way of eternal life.

Here again we find ourselves commending this young man. Here again he is a fine example. Here again we cannot but exclaim: "Oh that there were a like anxiety about spiritual realities on the part of the many to-day!"

Nor is even this all. See this rich young ruler's *uprightness*. When Jesus said: "Thou knowest the commandments—Do not commit adultery; Do not kill; Do not steal; Do not bear false witness; Defraud not; Honour thy father and mother;" he replied: "Master, all these have I observed from my youth." In answering thus he was speaking the honest truth according to his light; for according to his understanding of the Law, as prohibiting outward acts of sin, he had indeed "observed" all these things; and our Lord, therefore, did not contradict him. We may apply to this rich young man the words which Paul used to describe himself when formerly he was Saul the Pharisee —"Touching the righteousness which is in the Law, *blameless*." According to the school of the rabbis and the interpretations of the scribes, this young man wore "the white flower of a blameless life." What lacked he yet? Who could charge him with delinquencies? He was a model of religious seriousness and moral rectitude. Yes, indeed, here was a character of conspicuous uprightness! Many of those self-deceived persons of to-day who pretend that they do not *need* forgiveness through the precious blood of Christ or regeneration by the Holy Spirit are put to shame by the uprightness of this rich young ruler.

Just once more, see his *sincerity*. Jesus was greatly drawn to this young man. Mark says: "Then Jesus beholding him loved him." Our Lord, who "knew what was in man," saw the sincerity of this young man. He beheld in him the elements of a fine character—unspotted moral rectitude blended with aspiration for something nobler and higher and more spiritual. Here was something of real beauty and fair promise; and Jesus was drawn to it. "Jesus beholding him loved him."

There must have been something heart-melting about that love-look of Jesus. It was an earnest, tender, awful, searching look into this young man's soul. That love-look combined human sympathy with divine penetration. It was a divinely compassionate weighing of inner motives. It got right down to the very spirit of the man. There was only One who could look with such a look into a man's being; and even He, beholding this young man, "loved" him. Clearly then, the sincerity of this rich young ruler is beyond question.

Why, as we look on this nobleman we begin to fall in love with him ourselves. He has given us a succession of surprise after surprise, each new surprise revealing some commendable trait in his character. According to the verdict of Jesus Himself, there is only *"one thing"* which he lacks. Think of it—*"one thing"*! Most of us are conscious of lacking *many* things in our moral constitution. Could there be any finer commendation of this young man's character than for Jesus to say: *"One* thing thou lackest"? Truly we have good cause, so far, to sing this man's praises!

HIS PATHETIC BREAKDOWN

But now look at this rich young ruler's pathetic breakdown. Our Lord says to him: "One thing thou lackest: go thy way, sell whatsoever thou hast, and give to the poor, and thou shalt have treasure in heaven; and come, take up the cross, and follow Me." After the surprising succession of virtues which this young fellow has exhibited to us, we would expect him to have said: "Certainly, good Master; I will do this at once, even as Thou appointest." But *no!*—there is a sudden change: the ready tongue becomes dumb; the upturned gaze droops to the earth; the bended figure slowly rises; and with downcast head this rich young man—can it really be?—*slowly walks away!*

Mark says: "And he was sad at that saying, and went away grieved; for he had great possessions."

Oh, what a tragic anti-climax!—the man who came running now goes away with leaden footsteps; the ardent enquiry gives place to selfish refusal; the high aspiring becomes strangled by a secret but now suddenly exposed slavery to Mammon! The bright blue sky of youthful promise becomes suddenly overcast with dark cloud. The glorious rose which has just been opening out to full bloom now suddenly shrivels as though smitten by one awful breath of blight. Yes, there it is—"He was sad at that saying, and went away grieved; for he had great possessions." There is a sob in these words. We must read them with a heavy emphasis on that little word "was"—"and he *was* sad at that saying. . . ."

No doubt, too, there was a sob in this young man's heart as he turned away; but it was not the sob of the penitent; it was a strange tearless sob of selfish disappointment that he could not have eternal life without genuinely and absolutely yielding up everything to God. His sob was a mixture of grief and subtle anger arising from the sudden frustration of his secretly indulged hope that he could enter into the possession of salvation and yet somehow plausibly dodge the awkward discomfort of having his heart probed to its most sensitive and delicately camouflaged spot. He went away "grieved"—offended, cut to the quick; "for he had great possessions." He had been concerned to keep the commandments; but he was even more concerned to keep his money. He had bent the knee; but he would not bend his will. He had bowed his head, but not his heart. He had yielded obeisance; but he refused obedience. He had wanted heavenly treasures; but he could not give up earthly possessions. He knew what he *needed,* but would not forgo what he *wanted.* Christ called him to sacrifice the present for the future; but he sacrificed the future for the present. Christ called him to give up the material things which he possessed, for the one vital thing which he lacked; but he gave up the one thing that is vital for the many things that are vain. Christ's "Follow Me" called him to be an *apostle*; but he chose to be a *miser,* for he "went away" back to his "great possessions." He might have become an apostle Paul;

for he had great gifts and good education; but he turned away unsaved, confirmed in sin, hardened against what he knew to be the truth—with the result that he and his wretched money have never been heard of since.

Let us be quick to learn the lessons taught us by this young man's pathetic breakdown. The first is that *the salvation of the soul is not secured by so-called morality or good works or human merit*. This rich young ruler, as we have seen, was eager, reverent, courageous, discerning, spiritually inclined, morally upright, admittedly well-meaning, and, to crown all, highly religious—as is implied in his being a leader in the synagogue; yet his heart was not right with God and his soul was not saved.

The salvation of the soul comes by obeying the word of God in the Gospel, and by no other way. Had the rich young ruler lived in this gospel dispensation he would have been explicitly directed to believe on the Lord Jesus Christ, the Lamb of God, the world's great Sin-bearer. That is God's wonderful Gospel to us in this present day; and there is no other way whereby we may become saved. There must be an opening of the heart to the Saviour, and a yielding of the life to Him. Like the rich young ruler, we may be anxious about our salvation, we may be reverent toward Divine things, unashamed of our religious connection, spiritually inclined, morally upright, well-meaning, and highly religious; yet unless we have renounced all reliance upon these things for our soul's salvation, and have come to rely on Jesus alone, we are unsaved, for we are *sinners* needing pardon and cleansing and regeneration. No amount of so-called "good works" can cancel the sins we have committed, or wash our record white. No amount of religious observances can give us new hearts. But the moment we truly trust the Lord Jesus, who made atonement for us sinners, we are forgiven for *His* sake; and "the blood of Jesus Christ, God's Son, cleanseth us from all sin." Oh, we would plead now with every anxious soul —have done with trying to work out your own salvation by imaginary accumulations of merit. Fling such delusive endeavours to the moles and the bats. This very moment come as a self-confessed sinner and accept Jesus as Saviour. As the old Sankey's hymn says:

It is not thy tears of repentance nor prayers,
But the blood that atones for the soul;
On Him, then, Who shed it, thou mayest at once
Thy weight of iniquity roll.

Then take with rejoicing from Jesus at once
The life everlasting He gives;
And know with assurance thou never canst die,
Since Jesus, thy righteousness, lives.

Then, further, this rich young ruler illustrates to us *the self-ignorance which usually underlies the idea that we may be saved by our own morality*. Truly this young man was profoundly ignorant of his own heart; and so are all those unconverted persons who think to be justified by their own good works. When our Lord said: "Thou knowest the commandments: Do not commit adultery; Do not kill; Do not steal; Do not bear false witness; Defraud not; Honour thy father and mother;" He only mentioned those commandments which belong to what is called "the second table,"—that is, numbers 5 to 10, which concern our relationship toward our *neighbour*; and all *these* commandments refer to *conduct*. Therefore, inasmuch as this young man had refrained from any open or gross violation of these commands, he could say: "All these have I observed from my youth." It had not occurred to him that these commandments were meant to be applied to all his *thought* activity as well as to his outward acts,—that for instance even to *hate* a fellowman was an inward breach of the command against murder, and that to indulge even lustful *thought* was a breach of the command against adultery.

But the two greatest commandments in Israel's law were: "Thou shalt love the Lord thy God with all thine heart and with all thy soul and with all thy might"; and: "Thou shalt love thy neighbour as thyself." These two commandments go deep down underneath all mere *conduct* to our inmost *motives*. Our Lord had not mentioned these two basic and searching injunctions to the rich young ruler; but now, in the words "One thing thou lackest: go thy way, sell whatsoever thou hast, and give to the poor; and come, take up the cross, and follow Me," our Lord suddenly turns the penetrating light of this double commandment upon this young man, and tests him on this decisive point of self-sacrificing love to God and man. It is as though Jesus says to him: "Very well then, if you claim to have kept the commandments, *show* in a sacrificial way that your love of God is supreme in your life." At once the young man winces and recoils. The centre-nerve has been touched. He has been thinking himself thoroughly moral and upright; but now, in a flash, he sees his deep-down, ugly selfishness, his jealous reserve, and his cold, sinful alienation of heart from God. For the first time in his life he really sees himself; and he might well have cried out with young Isaiah, "Woe is me, for I am undone!"

Alas, such spiritual blindness as that in which this rich young ruler had lived is the commonest of things to-day. There are multitudes of self-righteous people who are profoundly ignorant as to the depth of their own sinfulness. They flatter themselves that they have not committed wicked deeds, that they have kept the commandments, that in fact they are to be commended for their goodness. They forget the holy nature of the God with whom they have to do. They forget how often they break the law in its spiritual sense, by pride and jealousy and anger and various forms of horrible selfishness; and most of all they fail to realise their alienation of heart from God—their lack of love to Him, their selfish reserve from Him, their independence of Him, their religious pride before Him. Oh, let us pray God to save us from this state of mind, this blind, stupid Phariseeism in which we place little value on the blood of Christ because we do not realise our desperate condition of sin and need! May the Holy Spirit show us our hearts as God Himself sees them, thus convincing us of our sin, and giving us no rest until we have washed away our sins in the precious blood of Christ!

There are many other lessons which we might draw from this case of the rich young ruler; but the one thing we would stress in closing is the solemn truth brought home to us in the words, "*one thing thou lackest.*" The one thing which is vitally and supremely urgent for all of us is the salvation of our souls by a true conversion to the Lord Jesus Christ. As it was with this rich young ruler of long ago, so there is usually some one special thing in the life which keeps us from coming to the Saviour. In the case of the rich young ruler it was his wealth. In our own case it may be something very different. Our Lord does not say to all who come to Him: "Sell what thou hast and give to the poor." He knew that money was this rich young man's special difficulty, and He therefore tested him on that very thing. Even so, the Lord Jesus knows all human hearts, and "needeth not that any should testify of man, for He knoweth what is in man" (John ii. 25): and Jesus knows what is in *your* heart and *mine*. He knows the thing which would keep us back, and He tests us on that very thing. There is no avoiding this. If He now puts His finger on that thing let us gladly yield it up rather than foolishly cling to it and finally perish. If we are willing to respond, then this very moment we may pass into joyous salvation and the possession of eternal life in Christ; for Jesus has said, once for all: "Him that cometh unto Me I will in no wise cast out"; and the Gospel message is: "Believe on the Lord Jesus Christ, and *thou shalt be saved.*" Yes, yes, this is "the one thing needful." Let us not turn away into the coldness and darkness as did the rich young ruler, but come with loving gratitude and simple-hearted faith to the gracious Saviour for His blood-bought gift of eternal life. God grant that we may all do this without delay!

THE MAN WHO KNEW HOW
LONG HE WOULD LIVE

SCRIPTURE SNAPSHOT

In those days was Hezekiah sick unto death. And Isaiah the prophet the son of Amoz came to him, and said unto him, Thus saith the Lord, set thine house in order ; for thou shalt die, and not live. Then Hezekiah turned his face to the wall, and prayed unto the Lord, and said, Remember now, O Lord, I beseech thee, how I have walked before thee in truth and with a perfect heart, and have done that which is good in thy sight. And Hezekiah wept sore. Then came the word of the Lord to Isaiah, saying, Go, and say to Hezekiah, Thus saith the Lord, the God of David thy father, I have heard thy prayer, I have seen thy tears ; behold, I will add unto thy days fifteen years. And I will deliver thee and this city out of the hand of the king of Assyria : and I will defend this city. And this shall be the sign unto thee from the Lord, that the Lord will do this thing that he hath spoken : behold, I will cause the shadow on the steps, which is gone down on the dial of Ahaz with the sun, to return backward ten steps. So the sun returned ten steps on the dial whereon it was gone down.—Isaiah xxxviii. 1–8 (R.V.).

THE MAN WHO KNEW HOW
LONG HE WOULD LIVE

GOOD king Hezekiah was a remarkable man. Soldier, states-
man, architect, poet, saint—he was all these; but there is also
a sense in which he was the most remarkable man who ever
lived. He was *the only man who ever knew for certain just when
he would not die, just how long he had to live!*

How this information came to him, and how he reacted to it,
and how it all eventuated—these form a unique episode in royal
biography. But there is more in it than that. Although scarcely
anybody may realize it, the repercussions from Hezekiah's extra
lease of fifteen years are felt among the nations to this very
day. In fact, the whole of Christendom has good cause to thank
God for that fig-poultice which miraculously healed the poorly
king of his complaint! We shall soon see why.

Moreover, this one and only mortal who foreknew the year
of his demise preaches certain big truths to us as *individuals,*
which we do well to ponder. Let us look up the records, then,
and see what we find. First of all we turn to Isaiah xxxviii. 1–8.
(See page across.)

Two very interesting questions are suggested to our minds by
this passage. First, did God have some special purpose in thus
lengthening Hezekiah's life? Second, how did Hezekiah use
those added fifteen years? The answer to the first question is:
Yes, God certainly had a special purpose in thus lengthening
Hezekiah's life. The answer to the second question is, that in
view of all the available data, Hezekiah used those added fifteen
years so profitably that we ourselves are still reaping the benefit
to-day. Everything we know about Hezekiah shows us that he
was the last man on earth simply to waste those years of special
grace on his own selfish interests. Read the noble account of
his early reign, in 2 Chronicles xxix. 1–11.

"Hezekiah began to reign when he was five and twenty years old, and he reigned nine and twenty years in Jerusalem. And his mother's name was Abijah, the daughter of Zechariah. And he did that which was right in the sight of the Lord, according to all that David his father had done. He, in the first year of his reign, in the first month, opened the doors of the house of the Lord and repaired them. And he brought in the priests and the Levites, and gathered them together into the east street, and said unto them: Hear me, ye Levites; sanctify now yourselves, and sanctify the house of the Lord God of your fathers, and carry forth the filthiness out of the holy place. For our fathers have trespassed, and done that which was evil in the eyes of the Lord our God, and have forsaken him, and have turned away their faces from the habitation of the Lord, and turned their backs. Also they have shut up the doors of the porch, and put out the lamps, and have not burned incense nor offered burnt-offerings in the holy place unto the God of Israel. . . . Now it is in mine heart to make a covenant with the Lord God of Israel, that his fierce wrath may turn away from us. My sons, be not now negligent; for the Lord hath chosen you to stand before him, to serve him, and that ye should minister unto him, and burn incense."

Then follows the account telling how, in obedience to Hezekiah's words, the temple was cleansed and reopened, and how Hezekiah restored the temple sacrifices and services. It was a wonderful time. The people evidently responded in good degree to the royal lead, for at the end of the chapter we are told how their freewill offerings were so plentiful that the depleted priesthood of the time were too few to cope with them. Next, in chapter xxx. comes the account of the great national Passover which Hezekiah caused to be held, and of which verse 26 says, "Since the days of Solomon, the son of David king of Israel, there was not the like in Jerusalem." Chapter xxxi. goes on to tell us how Hezekiah destroyed the idols and groves and false altars throughout the land of Judah, and how he brought about other long-needed religious reforms; and at the end of that chapter we read: "Thus did Hezekiah throughout all Judah, and wrought that which was good and right and truth before the LORD his God. And in every work that he began in the service of the house of God, and in the Law, and in the Commandments, to seek his God, *he did it with all his heart, and prospered.*"

These last-quoted words are fairly comprehensive. They make it quite clear that Hezekiah not only began well, but continued steadfastly afterward. This is corroborated by 2 Kings xviii. 5–8, where we have these notable words: "He trusted in the LORD God of Israel, so that after him was none like him among all the kings of Judah, nor any that were before him. For he clave unto the LORD, *and departed not from following Him,* but kept His commandments, which the LORD commanded Moses. And the LORD was with him, and he prospered whithersoever he went forth." One thing is very clear: Hezekiah was still closely following the Lord in the fourteenth year of his reign, just before the time when he became "sick unto death," and when the extra fifteen years were promised to him; for it was in that fourteenth year that the king of Assyria besieged Jerusalem, and Hezekiah's godly behaviour during that crisis was a shining example (see 2 Kings xix. 1–5, 14–19). Moreover, when Isaiah came to him with the words, "Set thine house in order, for thou shalt die, and not live," Hezekiah was able to say "Remember now, O LORD, how I have walked before Thee in truth and with a perfect heart" (Isaiah xxxviii. 3).

This, then, is the saintly king to whom that extra lease of fifteen years was extended. He was just the man to use those years for purposes of practical godliness. Let us look into those years, just a little. I think we shall make some interesting "finds."

First of all, it seems pretty certain that we owe, in good degree, to Hezekiah's activity during those years, *the arrangement and transmission of the Old Testament Scriptures.* That is a very big thing indeed to say when we remember the supreme preciousness of this dear old Bible of ours, with its vital message to human beings, and its vast impact upon human history. Yet it is true. Every time we read the Old Testament (which, let us never forget, is the foundation of the New) we are in debt to good king

Hezekiah and his men. Glance with me at certain evidences of Hezekiah's activities in connection with the Scriptures.

To begin with, mark his fine zeal for the *house* of Jehovah (2 Chronicles xxix. 3–19); then for the *worship* of Jehovah (verses 20–36). But now, in connection with his re-establishment of the temple services, we cannot fail to note his familiarity with, and strict adherence to, the Scriptures, or writings, concerning David's reign, three hundred years earlier. Glance down that twenty-ninth chapter of 2 Chronicles. In verse 25 Hezekiah sees to it that all the temple praise is "according to the commandment of David . . . and of the prophets." In verse 27 he commands that it shall be "with the *instruments* ordained by David." In verse 30 he commands that it shall be "with the *words* of David, and of Asaph the seer." Quite plainly, Hezekiah's delight was in the worship of Jehovah, and in the *word* of Jehovah. The sacred scriptures which had accumulated up to his own time were his guide and authority in all the service which he undertook. What is more, 2 Chronicles xxxi. 21 speaks of the *"work"* which he began, not only in "the service of the house of Jehovah," but also *"in the Law and in the Commandments."*

Nor is this all. It is certain that Hezekiah formed a *guild* of men specially set apart for such devout literary work. They are called "the men of Hezekiah." It is quite clear, for instance, that these "men of Hezekiah" had a good hand in the shaping of the Book of Proverbs into its present form. Turn to Proverbs xxv. 1, which marks the third of the three main divisions of that book. It says "These also are proverbs of Solomon, which the men of Hezekiah, king of Judah, copied out." This guild of copyists, transcribers and transmitters of the sacred text would scarcely begin and end their work simply with this one Book of Proverbs! Their work would extend to the other sacred writings; and Hezekiah himself would maintain a special interest in it, being chief supervisor of all their labours in the collecting and editing and arranging of the Scriptures. Probably leaders among "the men of Hezekiah" were "Shebna the scribe, and Joab the son of Asaph, the recorder" (2 Kings xviii. 18), and Isaiah the prophet. John Franklin Genung, in the International Standard Bible Encyclopædia, says the evidence is that "in Hezekiah's age, Israel reached its golden literary prime," with Hezekiah himself as the royal patron of piety and letters.

There seems to be a curious yet unmistakable confirmation of Hezekiah's work on the Scriptures, in the form of a certain peculiarity which very few people know about. At the end of many of the books of the Old Testament, in the Hebrew originals, three capital letters are found (three "majuscules" or majuscular letters, or "uncials," as they are called in palæographical terminology). No Hebrew transcriber and no compositor has dared to omit these three capital letters, even though not knowing their meaning. And so, although no one can tell us how they came to be there, or what they mean for certain, they still stand there, even to this day, transcribed and transmitted both in the manuscripts and even in the printed editions of the Hebrew Scriptures. And what *are* these three capital letters? They are the three Hebrew letters, Heth, Zayin, Qoph—in English, H, Z, K. These three letters are the first three in the Hebrew name of Hezekiah, and would well stand for an abbreviation of his name, in the same way that men put their *initials* on documents to-day. The late Dr. James W. Thirtle weightily suggested that nothing is more reasonable than to believe that when "the men of Hezekiah" completed their work of transcribing the different books, Hezekiah himself should have affixed his own sign-manual at the end, thus confirming their work by royal guarantee. The two or three other suggested explanations of these three capitals are so unlikely that they really lend further likelihood that these three "majuscules" are indeed Hezekiah's own sign-manual.

Now all these things point in one direction: Hezekiah and his guild of Hebrew literary experts had a great deal to do with the preserving and transmitting of the Old Testament Scriptures as they have come down to us to-day. Is this really surprising? Look a bit deeper. In Hezekiah's reign *the time had come when it was imperative that such a work should be done.* It was in Hezekiah's days, remember, that the ten-tribed northern kingdom, "Israel," were swept into captivity by the Assyrians, and dispersed among the cities of the Medes (2 Kings xviii. 11). Only the kingdom of Judah was now left, of which Hezekiah was king, at Jerusalem; *and even Judah's days were now numbered.* Only five more kings were to follow Hezekiah before Judah, too, would be plunged into the dark night of the Babylonian exile—and four out of those coming five were to prove ungodly failures. The moment had certainly come for the bringing together and the editing of the inspired Scriptures, with a view to their safe preservation and transmission. This great task would need Divine guidance. And if human instrumentality was to be used, who should be God's man for the purpose? Who was more suitable and willing than Hezekiah? And what time was more suitable than that of those God-given fifteen years? Hezekiah himself was warned, at the beginning of the added fifteen years, that ere long Judah would become prey to Babylon; and this would increase the good king's sense of the urgency of his sacred task. Yes, we have real reason to thank God for good king Hezekiah, that he was found so eminently worthy of those extra fifteen years, and that he did so much for posterity by his "work" in the Scriptures!

This brings us, in the second place, to a most intriguing further significance of those fifteen years. Along with Hezekiah's sickness and recovery, *they solve a problem which has baffled exegetes of the Old Testament for over two thousand years.*

Let me ask you to turn over to the Book of Psalms. There is one group of psalms which has always had a special interest. It consists of psalms cxx. to cxxxiv. These fifteen psalms are known to all of us as "The Songs of Degrees," because over each of them we find the title, "A Song of Degrees."

To what does this title refer? Well, that is just where all the haze and medley begins. An old Jewish notion was that these fifteen psalms were so-called because they were sung, each in order, on the fifteen steps of the Temple; but the difficulty is to prove that there ever *were* fifteen steps to the Temple! Nor do other suggested explanations fare much better.

Luther took the title as meaning "A Song in the higher choir," while Calvin thought it meant that these psalms were sung in a higher key. Bishop Jebb's idea was that these psalms were so-called because they were sung in connection with the "going up" of the Ark to Mount Zion. Other outstanding scholars, taking the Hebrew word as meaning *ascents* rather than "degrees," have supposed that a gradation, or series of ascents, in the poetic parallelism of these psalms is indicated, in which each line of a parallel carries the meaning of its predecessor a degree further or an ascent higher; but the difficulty about *this* supposed explanation is that not all these fifteen psalms possess this feature, while *other* psalms, besides these fifteen, *do* have this feature! Others again have suggested that these fifteen psalms were associated with Israel's going up to the three annual feasts at Jerusalem; but as one scholar points out, the majority of these psalms have, as it seems, "nothing at all" to do with pilgrimages! Yet again, the modern school makes all these psalms post-exilic, and tries to make out that they were songs of the exiles returning from the Babylonian captivity! Others spiritualise the psalms, and interpret them as referring to the Church; but the psalms themselves speak only of Israel, Judah, Jerusalem and Zion!

So there we are! Suggestions are plentiful; but does any one of those which we have mentioned commend itself as being the true explanation? The fact is that not one of the above "explanations" is the true one. For two thousand years, and maybe for two or three hundred years even more than that, the key to unlock these fifteen psalms has been lost, or, rather, to put it more truly, the key has lain there all the time, but has remained unrecognised and unused!

What, then, of these fifteen "Songs of Degrees"? Is there a really satisfactory solution? There is. Nor need we go outside the Bible to Tradition or to the Fathers or to human ingenuity. The explanation, as Dr. James W. Thirtle has shown, is inside the Bible itself.

The first thing to note is that the title, "A Song of Degrees," has the definite article, in the Hebrew, before that word "Degrees," and should therefore read: "A Song of THE Degrees." This at once suggests that certain well-known "degrees" are alluded to. Are there, then, any such mentioned in the Bible? There are; and they are the *only* "degrees" of which the Bible tells us. These were the degrees on the great sundial of King Ahaz, at Jerusalem. Like other such royal sundials of long-ago, the sundial of Ahaz would be an elaborate and very conspicuous edifice, with its scores of steps mounting up like a long, straight stairway, to a considerable height, and on which, step by step, or degree by degree, the shadow would be registered from the gnomon.

Are we told anything special about this sundial of Ahaz? We are: something *very* special. It was on this sundial, in the reign of Hezekiah, the son of Ahaz, that the shadow went back ten "degrees" or "steps," as a sign that fifteen years were to be added to Hezekiah's life! This supernatural happening is recorded in 2 Kings xx. 8–11 (which, please look up), where the word "degrees" is certainly given emphasis by repetition.

Is there any likelihood, then, that the "Songs of the Degrees" relate to Hezekiah and the degrees on the sundial of Ahaz? There is. We have seen that Hezekiah was the godliest of Judah's kings (2 Kings xviii. 5, 6) and that he was just the man, considered from a spiritual and literary point of view, to write such pieces as the "Songs of the Degrees." We have also seen that Hezekiah was very interested in psalms and spiritual songs, he being the king who restored the Temple worship, taking great care that all was done "according to the commandment of David" and "with the instruments ordained by David" and "with the words of David."

It is generally agreed by scholars that Hezekiah had a large part in shaping the Book of Psalms into its present form; and we have seen that the same is also true of the Book of Proverbs (Prov. xxv. 1). But, again, *Hezekiah was himself a psalm-writer*; for in Isaiah xxxviii., beginning at verse 9, *we find one of the psalms which he wrote*. What is still more striking is the reference, in that chapter, to *a set of "songs" composed by Hezekiah*. What "songs" could these be? It seems almost certain, from their connection, that they were the "Songs of the Degrees" which now appear in our Book of Psalms; for in verse 9 we are told that the psalm of Hezekiah which is there recorded was a "writing of Hezekiah, king of Judah, *when he had been sick, and was recovered of his sickness*" (the sickness in connection with which the shadow went back ten degrees: see v. 8); and at the end of that psalm Hezekiah says: "The Lord was ready to save me. Therefore we will sing *my songs* to the stringed instruments all the days of our life, in the house of the Lord" (v. 20).

Is still further evidence required? Then let us note that the number of the "Songs of the Degrees" is *fifteen*; and the number of years which were added to Hezekiah's life is also *fifteen*. The shadow went back *ten* degrees on the sundial; and *ten* of the "Songs of the Degrees" are left anonymous, while the remaining five are *not* left so, four being attributed to David, and one to Solomon. Reasons are not lacking why Hezekiah should leave *the ten by himself* without his name. A proper sense of humility would be enough, apart from anything else; and it may be that since the "songs" were known quite well to be Hezekiah's, the putting of his name with them was deemed to be quite unnecessary. It went without saying that they were his. He himself spoke of them as *"MY* songs",—as though, even then, they were already well known.

That they were carefully *arranged* into their present order is clear. There are five groups of three psalms each. In each group two are by Hezekiah, and one by David or Solomon. In each trio the first psalm is one of *trouble*; the second, one of *trust*; and the third, one of *triumph*.

But, added to all that we have said, the completing evidence that these fifteen "Songs of the Degrees" did indeed relate to Hezekiah and the degrees on the sundial, is the correspondence between their contents and the historical account, in Kings and Chronicles, of Hezekiah's illness and the siege of Jerusalem at that time by the Assyrian king. This, however, is a study in itself. We can only recommend here, "Trace out the correspondence yourself, as an interesting line of Bible study." If we relate those fifteen "Songs of the Degrees" to those extra fifteen years of Hezekiah, they will live for us in a new way. And let us not forget that here again is another precious legacy from those God-given fifteen years, a legacy for which we may well be grateful to this unique king who, alone among the sons of men, knew just how long he had to live!

And now, in the third place, let us draw a few very simple but weighty lessons of a practical kind from what we have found in connection with those fifteen years.

First, the unique fact that Hezekiah knew just how long he would live brings home to us the truth that *we ourselves have no such knowledge. We do not know at all how long we have*

to live, whether our remaining days on earth will be many or few.
Hezekiah was the only man who ever lived who knew for certain
that during a given period he would not die. So far as the rest of
us are concerned, the only thing about our life that is certain is
that it is *un*certain. Therefore we should see to it that our "house"
is always "set in order" in the sight of God. The thought of the
continual at-hand-ness of death should chasten all our behaviour.
To keep this thought in mind, in the right way, is not morbidity,
but wisdom. Not to take it into account, however common such
negligence may be, is a form of insanity due to hereditary sin and
the deceptions of the devil. The saintly Richard Baxter said that
he always preached as "a dying man to dying men" (was not that
one of the prime secrets of his power?). We dare not take to-
morrow for granted. We dare not presume on the future, lest a
voice should say to us, "Thou fool, this night thy soul shall be
required of thee." Especially in the supreme matter of our soul's
salvation let us not trade on any imaginary certainty that we
shall see to-morrow's sunrise. "Now," says the Scripture, is "the
accepted time." "To-day," says the Holy Spirit, if we will "hear
His voice." Be wise, unsaved one!—flee even now to Calvary,
that God-given refuge for sinners. See the Saviour there bearing
the world's sin, including yours and mine; and hear the word of
the Gospel—"Whosoever believeth on Him shall never perish,
but hath everlasting life." Nothing is more important than getting
right with God, and then living with our house "set in order."
A man of God, a certain Dr. Keen, lay dying. In the last three
days, when very sick, he never seemed able to pray once—not
in the strict sense of that term. Every gasp of his breath was,
"Blessed Jesus!" To an intimate friend at the bedside he said,
"Joseph, maybe you wonder why I am not praying at such a
serious time; but *there isn't any unfinished business.*" Let Hezekiah's extra lease, then, preach to us first of all the wisdom of
living with our house "set in order."

Second, we do well to reflect on the fact that *just as truly as
those extra fifteen years were a special gift of God to Hezekiah,
so are the days or years which we ourselves may yet live on earth.*
I rather think that one of the incidental reasons why God gave
those further years to Hezekiah was that we might see illustrated

the fact that it is God who portions out the lives of all human beings. Although no prophet comes to us, as Isaiah came to Hezekiah, to inform us how long we are yet to tenant the body, God none-the-less allots the number of years to each of us. What then shall I do with God's lease of years to me? I must take example from Hezekiah's use of those fifteen years which were given to him, and I must use every year that God gives me for purposes of practical godliness. I must count my life in terms of opportunity for serving God. I must "redeem the time" because "the days are evil." I heard a preacher say, recently, "Oh, I wish I had realized twenty years ago as keenly as I now do, that there is really no purpose in life, and nothing really worth living for, apart from the doing of the will of God." What real or worthy purpose *can* there be apart from the will of Him who made us? God help us to see it clearly—for everything depends on it— that life is vain and death is dark unless we live to fulfil the will of God!

We may draw a third lesson. As there was a great purpose running through Hezekiah's life, so there is an intended Divine purpose for each of our own; and, as Hezekiah's life was prolonged for the fulfilment of that purpose, so, *if we ourselves are truly living in and for the will of God, our life will be preserved until God's purpose through us is fully achieved.* This is really so. George Whitefield never said a truer thing than when, in the thick of persecution, he said, "I am immortal till my work is done." There is no such peace ever fills a human heart as that which comes when we are living out the motto: "The will of God, nothing less, nothing more, nothing else, and at all costs."

And again, as we think of those added fifteen years, let us thoughtfully observe *the efficacy of prayer in the life of the godly.* When Isaiah brought the message to Hezekiah, "Set thine house in order, for thou shalt die, and not live," Hezekiah was able to look up to God and say, "Remember now, O LORD, I beseech Thee, how I have walked before Thee in truth and with a perfect heart, and have done that which is good in Thy sight." The godly man knew full well that his standing before God was a matter of Divine grace and not of human merit; yet he knew also that there was a true sense in which he could make his sincere and steadfast godliness in past days the basis of his appeal to God: and God said, in effect, "Yes, Hezekiah, you are quite right; and I will do what you ask."

Prayer is still as efficacious in the life of the godly. Oh, it is a great thing, in time of crisis, to be able to call God to record that you have loyally walked with Him in the days that lie behind. When Hezekiah was stricken with his mortal sickness, a vast Assyrian army was before the gates of Jerusalem, preparing for assault. We can well understand Hezekiah's tears when, on top of this critical threat, he was told that he himself must prepare to die. But, in answer to Hezekiah's prayers, the Assyrian host was destroyed, and Jerusalem was saved, and Hezekiah's own life was extended for fifteen years! I believe in the operation of natural laws; but I believe that God reigns above all the laws by which He has conditioned the ongoing of the universe, and that He can answer the prayers of the godly in sovereign super-control. Human science deals only among second causes. He who is the First Cause can cverride all second causes if He so chooses, in the answering of prayer. Admittedly, God most often answers His people's prayers through ordinary means; but we must not *limit* Him to such procedure, despite the affirmations of modern science. In His providential government of this world, the Almighty leaves Himself free to answer the prayers of the godly by any means which He chooses, whether natural or supernatural.

Let the godly Hezekiah stand before us, then, as a striking example of the efficacy of prayer in the life of the godly. It is not enough, of course, just to turn to God in a crisis. That is why many of the excited prayers of people who suddenly find themselves in straits are not answered.

There are other practical lessons, too, lying before us in connection with those extra fifteen years of Hezekiah; but we must leave them.

We have found enough already, however, to challenge our minds and urge us to truer godliness in the days which may still be allotted to us. The supreme lesson of Hezekiah, and those fifteen years which glorified his reign, is *the worthwhileness of godliness.*

THE MAN WHO LED PAUL
TO CHRIST

SCRIPTURE SNAPSHOT

Now there was a certain disciple at Damascus, named Ananias : and the Lord said unto him in a vision, Ananias. And he said, Behold, I am here, Lord. And the Lord said unto him, Arise, and go to the street which is called Straight, and inquire in the house of Judas for one named Saul, a man of Tarsus ; for behold, he prayeth ; and he hath seen a man named Ananias coming in, and laying his hands on him, that he might receive his sight. But Ananias answered, Lord, I have heard from many of this man, how much evil he did to Thy saints at Jerusalem : and here he hath authority from the chief priests to bind all that call upon Thy name. But the Lord said unto him, Go thy way : for he is a chosen vessel unto Me, to bear My name before the Gentiles and kings, and the children of Israel : for I will show him how many things he must suffer for My name's sake. And Ananias departed, and entered into the house ; and laying his hands on him said, Brother Saul, the Lord, even Jesus, who appeared unto thee in the way which thou camest, hath sent me, that thou mayest receive thy sight, and be filled with the Holy Ghost. And straightway there fell from his eyes as it were scales, and he received his sight ; and he arose and was baptized ; and he took food and was strengthened.

—Acts ix. 10–19 (R.V.).

THE MAN WHO LED PAUL
TO CHRIST

"There was a certain disciple at Damascus, named Ananias."
—Acts ix. 10.

THERE was a task needing to be done. Someone was needed to do it. The Master looked for someone. He found His man—ready, willing, faithful. That man was Ananias. He was the right man in the right place at the right time; and God used him. The outcome was incalculable blessing.

Ananias is a most inspiring pattern of Christian godliness, not so much for preachers or other public workers as for the generality of disciples who, like himself, are called to live the Christian life amid the ordinary circumstances of work-a-day life. How many there are who long to live at their very best for Christ, but feel that their circumstances keep them hidden away in an obscurity which prevents their being used for Him!

The ordinary life is often the most difficult. It has the fewest outward stimulants, and therefore requires a deeper and steadier faith within the heart. We need Christians who will live the ordinary life in a really out-of-the-ordinary way. Our Lord has a special pleasure, as He Himself has said, in those of His servants who are "faithful over a *few* things." We should beware of misappreciating or undervaluing the so-called commonplace. It is the aggregate of commonplace things which constitutes the greatest of all influences in the history of mankind.

> "A commonplace life," we say, and we sigh;
>   Yet why should we sigh as we say?
> The commonplace sun in the commonplace sky
>   Makes lovely the commonplace day.

The moon and the stars, they are commonplace things,
The flower that blooms, and the robin that sings;
Yet sad were the world, and unhappy our lot,
If flowers all failed and the sunshine came not!
And God, who considers each separate soul,
From commonplace lives makes a beautiful whole.

To all those Christian believers who feel that there is a disappointing sense of ordinariness about their life and surroundings, this man, Ananias, is a silver starlight of encouragement. He is mentioned only twice in the New Testament—in the ninth and twenty-second chapters of the Acts of the Apostles; and even in these two places he is only introduced in a rather incidental way. Yet he amply shows us how the glory of the upper world may be brought to flash upon the dismal details of "the common round and the daily task."

Look, then, for a few moments, at this man, Ananias, and see in him a sparkling gem of Christian discipleship. There are three radiant characteristics which gleam forth for our inspiration— his readiness, his willingness, his faithfulness. How often we fail because of breakdown in one or other of these three qualifications! Perhaps we may learn much from Ananias. Let us see.

HIS READINESS

See his *READINESS*. We are told three things about him. First, he is simply called *"a certain disciple"* (Acts ix. 10). He was neither an apostle nor a great preacher; nor does he appear to have been a leader or an official or even an outstanding personality. Likely enough we should never have heard anything about him had it not been for his figuring in Saul's conversion. How heartening to know that *God* knew all about him! No depth of obscurity can hide us from *His* gracious gaze. "The Lord knoweth the way of the righteous." Ananias is like some unknown star which for a brief spell reveals itself to the eye of the telescope and then forever disappears again. He was just an ordinary, humble disciple, who evidently sought to glorify Jesus by a consecrated life amid the unexciting usualness of customary Damascus ways and doings.

Second we are told that he was *"a devout man according to the law"* (Acts xxii. 12). That is saying a good deal. See here his devotion to principle. He was so honest and religiously particular that he could endure the microscope where perhaps others of a more imposing outward profession would wince. He was principled to the last detail. As a true Christian and a loyal Jew together he could not be otherwise. Nothing was morally unimportant with him. I wish that many of us who profess the name of Jesus to-day were similarly principled in our domestic and business and recreational relationships. Our devotion to that which is highest should show itself everywhere in our life.

Third, Ananias had *"a good report of all the Jews that dwelt there."* Here learn something of his discreetness. I imagine that the Damascus Jew would not have eulogised Ananias overmuch, remembering his attachment to the sect of the crucified Nazarene, unless he had been winsomely discreet in his Christian piety and witness! It is no small thing to have our character praised by those who strongly differ from us. Such a reputation as Ananias had is not gained in five minutes or nine days. It is evident that he was thoroughly well-known in Damascus. He had been there a long while and was probably a native of the place. He was thought well of by those with whom he lived and worked and transacted business—and that, not for a week or two only, but month after month. Such men are grand sermons. Oh, for volumes of them! Such life-sermons are incalculably more telling and convincing than mere lip-advertisements. In an environment as drab as, if not drabber than, our own, this disciple of Jesus lived excellently. In one sense, he was a Mr. Nobody; but in the far higher sense, he was one of the aristocracy of heaven!

HIS WILLINGNESS

But look now at Ananias's *willingness*. Think you it was an easy thing which the Master set His servant to do when he said: "Arise, and go into the street which is called Straight, and enquire in the house of Judas for one called Saul of Tarsus"? Be under no such impression. Ananias had not been deserving of overmuch blame had he shrunk away in fear from such an ordeal. Was not Saul the most virulent and notorious oppressor of the Christians in all Judaea? Had he not come to Damascus, even at this very time, on a blood-curdling excursion of anti-Christian persecution? How dare Ananias fling himself into the eager clutches of this infuriated ringleader of the Saviour's adversaries? Must the lamb walk into the very mouth of the lion? Could it be of any imaginable use to preach Calvary to *this* hot-blooded, hard-hearted, implacable foe of the Nazarene? Could such an Ethiopian *ever* change his skin? But the Lord said to him: "Go thy way, for he is a chosen vessel unto Me, to bear My Name before the Gentiles and kings and the children of Israel; for I will show him how great things he must suffer for My Name's sake." Without further demur, "Ananias went his way." He willingly obeyed!

Ananias was obedient as to *time,* as to *place,* as to *result.* He was willing to go just when and just where the Master directed, and to count on his Lord's faithfulness as to the result. Time, place, result—these are just the three points on which most of ourselves dare to have foolish controversy with our Lord; and it is due to this that we miss the joy of fellowship with Him in our own service. We do well to learn from Ananias the lesson of yielding exact obedience to our Master.

HIS FAITHFULNESS

Now see Ananias's *faithfulness.* In the obedience of Ananias there shines a beauteous triple fidelity—the fidelity of Christian love, Christian loyalty, and Christian humility. His Christian *love* is seen in his attitude towards Saul. He goes in to the arch-persecutor with the eloquently affectionate greeting "Brother Saul!" Moreover, "he put his hands on him,"—a very gracious act, for, whereas Saul had come to lay the hand of violence on Ananias, Ananias now lays the gentle hand of brotherliness on Saul! There is not a trace of resentment in the entire demeanour of Ananias. Christian love displays itself in gracious, fullest victory.

But if his Christian love is revealed in his attitude towards Saul, his *loyalty* is seen in his attitude towards his Lord. His first word, after saluting Saul, is: "The Lord, even Jesus . . . hath sent me." Ananias would not let his expression of brotherliness towards Saul cause him to shrink from affirming the LORD-SHIP OF JESUS, even though that was the very thing against which Saul had been so madly fighting. So, after saying *"Brother Saul,"* he immediately proceeds, *"THE LORD, EVEN JESUS . . . hath sent me."* Choice blend of discretion and devotion!

See here, also, this good man's *humility*. He did not obtrude himself into his message. The very opposite was the case. His only reference to himself was the only one that was needful—"The Lord, even Jesus . . . hath sent me." He did not start explaining who or what he was. He was content to be the faithful anonymous messenger of his Master.

Admire, then, the exemplary faithfulness of Ananias—his Christian love, loyalty, lowliness.

This was the man God used: ready, willing, faithful! Yet just an ordinary, humble, obscure working man. As to his *readiness,* we mark his discipleship, devotedness, discreetness. As to his *willingness,* we mark his obedience concerning time and place and result. As to his *faithfulness,* we mark his Christian love and loyalty and lowliness. This is the kind of servant God always uses.

SOME PRACTICAL APPLICATIONS

Christian disciple, never complain that your circumstances render a robust Christian life and witness impossible. Do your difficulties and discouragements seem like immovable mountains? God says to you through His prophet, "I will make all My mountains a way" (Isaiah xlix. 11). Does your sky seem all grey and cloudy? Clouds are only dark and drab until the sun glorifies them. In the large majority of cases, circumstances are only imaginary prison bars. When our hearts are genuinely yielded to Christ, we hear a soul-thrilling voice through the dull bars that have apparently confined us—"Behold, I have set before thee an open door, and no man can shut it!" Instead of seeing a difficulty in every opportunity, we then see an opportunity in every difficulty. Instead of seeing thorns with every rose, we see a rose with every thorn. Let the glad cry of the imprisoned Paul come to our ears, from behind *real* prison bars—"I can do all things through Christ which strengtheneth me!"

We are not just toying with words when we say that there is a real sense in which Christian believers need never be "under the circumstances." The indwelling Saviour can give us a liberating independence of exterior environment. Nor need we live "in the limelight" to do true service for our heavenly Master. It is not only the front line of organ pipes that give forth music. Some of those out of sight are just as musical and sometimes are more important. A rose need not be seen before its fragrance can be appreciated. The longer I live, the more do I perceive the power and value of those lives which, although they never find mention in newspaper columns, transmit the love and life and grace of Christ among neighbours and workmates and friends in the ordinary walks of life.

> If this bit of earth may be
> Stronger for the strength I bring,
> Sweeter for the songs I sing,
> Happier for the path I tread,
> Lighter for the light I shed,
> Richer for the gifts I give,
> Purer for the life I live,
> Nobler for the death I die,
> Not in vain have I been I.

No, publicity is not an essential either to faithfulness or to true success. Service in secret often has "house top" results, though the connection may not always be detected. We may feel out of sight, but we are never out of *God's* sight. His love-look is ever on us. He is watching, to see whether, Ananias-like, we are faithful in our present circumstances. He may have much wider fields of service for us in the future; but the determining factor is fidelity in the present.

Refuse to be the slave of circumstance! Through faith and prayer and consecration and a humble claiming of the Holy Spirit's power, transform the difficulties into opportunities. Remember that our truest service for Christ is not that which

we merely do *for* Him, but that which we allow *Him* to do *through*
us. Christian service is not a matter of indefatigable doing, doing,
doing. Far more vital than what we do is what we *are*. However
true and important it may be in other connections, it is most of
all emphatic here, that *quality* rather than quantity is the thing
that really tells. Five words, shot through with the love of Christ
and the fire of Pentecost, from the lips of a sanctified disciple,
will accomplish more, in a spiritual and regenerating sense, than
five thousand sermons or lectures delivered merely in the energy
of the flesh. That is not just word play. It is fact. Most of us
think we believe it; but I wonder if we actually do? In the truest
and highest sense, service for Christ is not mere physical activity,
or even mental productivity, but *conductivity*. We are not called
to be creators, but *transmitters*. Fundamentally, the world does
not need you or me; but it desperately needs Christ. We are
meant to be transmitters of His life and love and saving grace
to others.

> Oh, to be nothing, nothing,
>   Simply to lie at Thy feet,
> A broken and emptied vessel,
>   For my Master's use made meet!
> Emptied that Thou mayest fill me,
>   As forth to Thy service I go;
> Emptied, that so unhindered,
>   Thy life through mine might flow!

Think again of that dear man, Ananias. Live for Christ at
your very best, just where you are, and a day at a time. Do
you seek to live a holy life, and find it impossible? Well, do not
try to live a holy *life*: live a holy *minute*! Sixty of them make
a holy *hour*! As the well-known hymn says, "Take *time* to be
holy." When I was minister of Bethesda Free Church, Sunder-
land, I used to hear grateful references to a deacon of that church
who had died some years before I went there. What a fragrant
memory he had left! His participation in the office-bearers' meetings, his very presence, and his prayers had been a lasting bene-
diction. He had always brought an unmistakable sense of God's
presence. What was his secret? Well, he was Mr. W. D. Long-

staff; and it was he who wrote that hymn to which we have just referred—"Take time to be holy." Let us not rashly blurt out that we simply cannot make time, for, remember, we are dealing with *GOD*. And besides, do we not simply insist on making time for other things of far less importance? I know we cannot do what is not possible; but if we were to make the matter one of strict conscience, not to say of loving devotion, between our Lord and ourselves, oh, what a difference there would soon be in many of us! We would become "vessels unto honour, sanctified, and meet for the Master's use, and prepared unto every good work" (2 Tim. ii. 21). It was because Ananias was such a vessel—"prepared" and *ready for use,* that the Master used him as He did, in connection with Paul.

What sort of a vessel would we ourselves use in an emergency? A draught of water is needed immediately for some unexpectedly ailing person. There are two vessels at hand. One is a beautifully wrought silver chalice; the other is a plain earthenware cup with the handle broken off. Outwardly there is no comparison. The costly silver chalice at once takes the eye. But on being picked up and quickly examined, it is found to be dirty inside, with the dust and stains of years; and there is no time to give it the thorough cleansing which it needs. The plain earthenware cup is picked up instead. It is beautifully clean, not a suggestion of dust or defilement; and at once it fulfils the purpose, because it is *ready for use* just when wanted. I wish we could all learn this lesson with deep and lasting definiteness.

Christian disciple, seek no longer the elaborate and spectacular forms of service for Christ. Seek sanctification, purity of heart, humility of spirit, preparedness for any and every sudden call of our heavenly Master. Seek to distil the fragrance of the Rose of Sharon in your present environment. If you glorify God to-day, just where you are, there is no telling how He may glorify you to-morrow. In the most unlikely surroundings there are opportunities for serving Christ as plentiful as daisies and buttercups in the meadows during the summer months. We have all heard of the farmer who for the first time saw the beauty of a bluebell under the microscope. He almost looked his eyes out; and then with a tear dripping down each cheek, he exclaimed, "Heaven forgive me; I've trodden on thousands!" If only we have eyes to see we soon find it is the same with opportunities: they are everywhere. By how we live, by what we do, by words we speak, by looks and tones, by our actions and reactions, by discreet witness for Christ, by visits, by tracts, by prayer, by these and those and the other ways, we may be making a contribution to the eternal wellbeing of souls every hour that we live.

No, a thousand times, service for Christ does not depend on publicity! More than ever, in these days, the propagation of the Gospel depends upon the Ananiases. It is only the rank and file of Christian believers who can bridge the widening gulf between the pulpit and the public. Let each Christian say at the beginning of each new day, "Much depends on me to-day, in the interests of my Lord." Some time ago a speaker over the radio was telling of his visit to a large munitions factory during the war. He said that the first thing which impressed him as he approached the factory was a word painted in huge, bright letters on the main gate. The word was *IADOM*. It puzzled him, but he thought no more of it until a little later when he was looking through the interior of the factory. There, on every wall, and in every window, the same word appeared. "Iadom," he said to himself, "that's a new one for me. I'm a university man, and have learned several languages, but I don't recall anything like *Iadom* before!" He did not like to ask the meaning of it, lest he might be betraying a needless ignorance; but he felt rather annoyed with himself for not knowing. However, after his tour of inspection, a dainty little typist who directed him back to his car, happened to say, "You noticed our motto, of course!" Rather shamefacedly he replied, "Yes." "I suppose you know what it means?" she asked. He was obliged now to confess his ignorance. "Oh, it's quite simple," she replied with a smile, "the letters stand for, *'It All Depends On Me'*." I.A.D.O.M. "It all Depends On Me." Did ever the human race get such a lesson on the strategic value of the individual as in the last war? Somehow, in that "total war" everything depended on the fitness and loyalty and morale of the individual. It is the same in "the holy war" which we wage for Christ against sin and Satan. Each one, even the obscurest, is of incalculable importance.

Most of the biographies which we read are those of outstanding *leaders,* and naturally they are of most interest to those who in their own turn are called to leadership. But Ananias, as we said at the beginning, is an example to the rank and file of our Lord's army. Mark this man. We do well to take a good, long, thoughtful look at him. He can teach us the secret of making the secular sacred, the commonplace beautiful, and the earthly heavenly.

Let Ananias, with his readiness for service, be an example to us. Let his consistent godliness be an incitement to us to live similarly. Let his readiness, willingness, faithfulness, be both a pattern and an inspiration. Let the beautiful way in which Christ used this ordinary and perhaps obscure man give such solid comfort to us as shall cause us to resolve on fuller loyalty to our heavenly Master in the days ahead. Thus, the common round and the daily task will become transfigured.

"Glory amid drudgery"!—
——Myriad household cares!
Washing, cleaning, mending,—
——Sweeping down the stairs,
Things I well might chafe at,
Dull and drab and drear,
How mid these is glory?
Where does it appear?

In HIS service royal,
Could our eyes but see,
Each who serves is given
Royal livery;
In life's humblest station,
Doing lowliest things,
Glory gilds all service
For the King of kings.

THE MAN WHO HELPED
CARRY THE CROSS

SCRIPTURE SNAPSHOTS

THIS IS WHAT MATTHEW SAYS:—

And as they came out, they found a man of Cyrene, Simon by name ; him they compelled to bear His Cross.—Matthew xxvii. 32.

THIS IS WHAT MARK SAYS:—

And they compel one Simon, a Cyrenian, who passed by, coming out of the country, the father of Alexander and Rufus, to bear His cross.—Mark xv. 21.

THIS IS WHAT LUKE SAYS:—

And as they led Him (Jesus) away, they laid hold upon one Simon, a Cyrenian, coming out of the country, and on him they laid the cross, that he might bear it after Jesus.—Luke xxiii. 26.

THE MAN WHO HELPED
CARRY THE CROSS

"On him (Simon) they laid the cross, that he might bear it after Jesus."—Luke xxiii. 26.

THIS INCIDENT in connection with our Lord's crucifixion is familiar to all readers of the New Testament. It is presumably of special noteworthiness, for all three synoptists draw attention to it; and, as in other such cases, there is much point in collating the respective references in Matthew, Mark, and Luke.

Each of the three verses (Matt. xxvii. 32, Mark xv. 21, Luke xxiii. 26) may seem brief enough in itself, yet the three together make a most informing and significant trio. They strike connections with other Scriptures, and open up quite fascinating avenues of enquiry. Metaphorically, they "lift up the curtain" on three successive scenes in what we may call the drama of Simon the Cyrenian.

SCENE 1: A SAD WONDER

It is between nine and ten o'clock on a Friday morning, the 15th day of the month Nisan, that is, the 11th day of April, in the year A.D. 32, according to Julian reckoning. We are standing by the city gate of old-time Jerusalem. From within the city strange cries and sounds of commotion fall on our ears. A little later there slowly emerges a strange procession, or, rather, a slow-moving, noisy medley of people, and a ghastly sight which chills the heart. It is a disorderly crowd, some gloating and shouting, some weeping and wailing, others jabbering and questioning, all jostling each other round a condemned criminal who is being led out to be crucified!

How sickeningly out-of-keeping it seems with the beauty and freshness of the morning, and with the great religious festival now being celebrated in Jerusalem, to which devout Jews have gathered from all parts of the world! And what peculiarly concentrated interest many of this strangely mixed crowd are showing in this criminal!

They have reached the gates now. Why, many of Israel's best-known religious leaders are in that motley mix-up! And what expressions are on their faces! Those black, beady eyes, how they gleam with malicious gratification! Those hard-set Jewish features, how tightened up they now are into relentless cruelty which there is no attempt to conceal! As they snap out taunts and gibes, many of them are for all the world like hounds, yapping and yelping to get at their prey and tear it to pieces! But there are others in that throng, with a very different expression from that of those Pharisees and Sadducees. The pallor of alarm is on their faces. There are some younger men there who seem to know the prisoner well; their eyes carry that strained look which betokens stunning dismay and intense sympathy. There is a noticeable percentage of women there, too, red-eyed, blanch-cheeked, with frightened glances now and then at the soldiers, but with ever-reverting gaze of yearning but frustrated compassion towards that doomed man. And there are the Roman soldiers—the "centurion" and his "quaternion" of brawny soldier-executioners, who every now and then clout the head of an unwary intruder who gets in the way and impedes their progress with the prisoner.

And there, in the middle, is the prisoner Himself. Amid the rabble cries of the crowd, the gruff voices of the soldiers can be heard urging Him forward; but He cannot increase the pace. He drags His limbs along in an almost fainting condition. Streaks and patches of blood show through His garment where His skin has been lacerated by severe whipping. There is a trail of blood on the ground. He must be still bleeding under His clothes. There seem to be spiky thorns, also, sticking in His hair. There has evidently been some coarse horse-play with this prisoner. There are still bleeding cuts across His forehead. His face is bruised and swollen and discoloured here and there from heavy blows struck with clenched fists. Slung round His neck is the tablet inscribed with the crime for which He dies. It says that this is "Jesus, the king of the Jews"! Strange king this!

It seems almost too much for Him to hold Himself up, but to have to struggle forward bearing the long, heavy beam and transom which are to be nailed together and made into His cross at Golgotha is more than He can now accomplish. It is scarcely a quarter of a mile from the city-gate to that knoll, but He just cannot reach it—not, at least, without some assistance in the dragging of that grim burden. He halts, He sways, He is about to fall; but a rough hand steadies Him, and He limps another pace or two. Again He staggers; He sinks down under the beam and cross-bar. The soldiers are getting impatient; they want the job over; they look round to commandeer some onlooker for the job of assisting the prisoner.

Oh, what a touching commentary it is on the sufferings of our dear Lord, that another must thus help Him carry His cross! And what an indictment of the judicial authorities, that they should have sponsored such brutal ill-treatment of so inoffensive a defendant as Jesus, before ever the crucifixion itself was perpetrated! The Saviour must certainly have been near the point of exhaustion; and little wonder, after His "agony" in Gethsemane, His wrestle with the powers of darkness, His sweat of blood, His nocturnal arraignment and rough-handling before Caiaphas, His early morning examination before Pilate, His later ill-usage by king Herod and the royal men-at-arms, His further trial before Pilate, the excruciating scourging, the purple robe, the crown of thorns, the brutal mauling at the hands of the Prætorium guards, the loss of blood, the lack of food and drink and sleep, and beside all these things, that most mysterious and awful suffering of all, the now-intensifying consciousness of the world's vast and deadly sin-burden crushing down upon Him as our Substitute and Sinbearer.

Yes, all this has preceded that early-morning scene at the city gate, as the patient but now fainting Jesus of Nazareth struggles painfully forward, bearing that heavy beam and cross-bar to Calvary. There is not a glint of sympathy, however, in the eyes of those soldiers, as they now look round impatiently to seize on someone to help the prisoner. They simply want to get the job over quickly for their own sake; and, by one of those tantalising minor ironies which mock us all at times, they chance to fix their eyes on someone who was not following the crowd at all, but was on his way into Jerusalem for worship, and had simply paused for a moment to see what this early-morning rabble was about. This ˙was Simon of Cyrene.

The soldiers neither knew nor cared who he was, though even *they* might have shown a little considerateness if they *had* known. Matthew, Mark, and Luke all tell us that he was a Cyrenian, that is, he was from Cyrene, which was the chief city of the Roman colony of Libya in North Africa. There were large numbers of Jews in those parts, as Josephus tells us. The Cyrenian Jews, along with Alexandrian Jews and others, seem to have had a special synagogue of their own at Jerusalem (Acts vi. 9); and batches of them would travel the hundreds of miles each year by land or sea, to be present at the great annual religious festivals in Jerusalem. Some of the wealthier Jews perhaps would come the long distance each year; but many others with less means would save up for years for such a visit to the holy city. We do not know to which class Simon belonged, though probably it was to the better class, if we may judge from certain hints which we shall mention later. Even so, it may easily be that this visit of Simon to the Jewish capital, for the annual Passover and Pentecost celebrations, was the fulfilling of a long-cherished dream. Certainly, Cyrene was a long, long way off, and few, if any, at that Passover, had come a greater distance than he. From Mark we learn that he was a married man with a family. His wife and sons would be away back home in Cyrene; and Simon would be storing his mind with many interesting things to tell them on his return. Little did he anticipate the experience which was now coming to him on this Friday morning!

From his coming into the city at an early hour for worship, we judge him to have been a devout and zealous man. Two of the Gospel writers say that he was "coming *out of the country*," that is, from one of the outside districts where, probably, he had his lodgings during the Jerusalem celebrations. Mark tells us that he would have "passed by"—anxious to avoid such an unseemly sight as this, of a felon being taken out to be crucified. From these and other stray hints we infer that Simon was of the devout, decorous, and sensitive type, just the last sort of person to enjoy being mixed up with a gory crucifixion affair. Perhaps it was because he had never seen a crucifixion before that he just paused for one moment and peered into that ring, intending to pass on at once; but that one moment was fatal. All in a matter of seconds, the unwary man found himself plunged into the most horrible ordeal of his life!

Get the scene, then, and try to enter into Simon's reactions. He draws near the gates, his mind occupied with godly contemplations and pleasant anticipations of the great gatherings soon to be held in the city. Just at the same moment this strangely mixed crowd of high and low, rich and poor, learned and illiterate, gloatingly vociferous and mournfully wailing people also reaches the gates, with the pathetic figure of Jesus in the middle, struggling forward under the weight of that heavy beam and crossbar. Simon gives a shudder at the unexpected spectacle, and wishes he had never seen it; yet it is so arresting, that somehow he cannot help momentarily pausing to look. Almost before he realizes that the crowd has spread around him, a heavy hand slaps his shoulder, and a raucous voice commands, "Shoulder that cross!" Oh! the ghastly insult of it! The sickening repulsiveness of it! What revulsion he feels! He is unwilling (Matthew and Mark both say that he had to be "compelled," indicating resistance). He struggles to get away, but those strong hands tighten their grip on him (Luke says they "laid hold" on him, as though he made to struggle free). What a shame-facing disgrace he feels it, to be so conspicuously and humiliatingly mixed up in this abhorrent affair, this public execution by the most execrable and torturous of all forms of execution, this public crucifixion of one who must be some notorious murderer! Oh, to be so suddenly and helplessly mixed up with a ghastly incident like this!—to have to walk with the criminal himself in the middle of this mob —and worst of all, to have to carry the very cross! He turns sickly at the sight of the heavy beam and the blood-drops on the roadway! He suddenly thinks of those away back at home: if *they* knew what was happening! What would they say when he told them afterward! No! he cannot do this thing! Why should the soldiers pick on *him*? He struggles; he protests; but it is useless; struggling is only making things worse. Despite all his expostulation he finds himself forced to submit. And so, with face alternately crimson and pale, head hung low, Simon bends beneath that wooden beam, and slowly follows the prisoner.

Then, something happens which completely changes Simon's feelings, and stirs strange new emotions within him. The informal procession is now away from the city gates. The noisy clamour and excited jabber subsides somehow as the brow of the crucifixion hillock comes into view. And more clearly now, the wailing of the *women's* voices can be heard, for (as Luke xxiii. 27 tells us) there is "a great company" of women in that crowd, who "bewail" and "lament" Jesus. Simon becomes aware that the prisoner, who is just in front of him, at the fore end of the beam, wishes to stop. Yes, Jesus halts, then turns and speaks to the women: "Daughters of Jerusalem, weep not for Me, but for yourselves and your children. . . ." In that interval Simon catches a heart-moving glimpse of the most wonderful man he has ever seen. Forgetting, for a tense moment, the indignity of his humiliating position, he gazes, rapt, at that face. Surely this is no ordinary criminal. No! A thousand times No! Never has he seen so noble a brow, so kingly and yet so kindly a face, such eyes—flashing with fiery majesty yet with exquisite tenderness and sympathy. Somehow the blood and thorns and bruises only enhance the strange fascination of that face. Oh, the gentle, thrilling power of that personality!—the mingled dignity and humility of His bearing!—the rich, full sympathy of His voice and words! —the calm self-possession!—the strong, noble manliness!—the impression of utter purity! And, as Jesus finishes speaking to the women, ere He turns again towards Calvary, He looks on Simon—oh, such a look; a never-to-be-forgotten look! It is a haunting look, a searching, compassionate, reassuring look; a look of utter understanding and sympathy; a look of such melting, thrilling power as only Simon himself ever knew! After this, Simon carries the cross with very different feelings.

SCENE 2: A GLAD WONDER

Seven weeks have slipped away. Simon's long-contemplated visit to Jerusalem is nearly over; but having come so far he cannot think of leaving before the Pentecost celebrations, fifty days after the Passover.

Never has a day passed since that indelible Friday morning without that cross-bearing experience recurring to his thoughts or cropping up in conversation. He has learned a great deal since then about this remarkable young prophet of Galilee, this Jesus of Nazareth whose cross he helped to carry; and the more he has heard the more he has wanted to hear. He has heard Him discussed on every hand. Despite the fact that He was crucified as an abhorred criminal, the common people seem to think there was nobody like Him. Again and again Simon hears of the remarkable purity of His character, yet of His friendliness with tax-gatherers and those who had gone wrong, and of His wonderful sympathy with all those in trouble. Many of His amazing miracles are related, and some of His remarkable parables are recounted.

Furthermore, for days now there have been strange rumours about the disappearance of the corpse from the sepulchre, even though the sepulchre had been sealed, and a watch set at the request of the chief priests, because they remembered Jesus having said he would rise again on the third day (Matt. xxvii. 62–66). It seems *certain* that the body *did* disappear, but *how* is something of a mystery. The chief priests are now saying that some of the disciples of Jesus came by night and stole the body away while the guards were asleep (Matt. xxviii. 11–15). But how did they break the seal and remove the body and get away without disturbing the guards? And how did they manage to remove the huge boulder which had been forced into the mouth of the sepulchre? And why were all the soldiers guilty of being asleep when they should have been on guard?

There is something strange about it all. The chief priests seem uneasy; and the soldiers themselves, so Simon heard, had seemed pretty vague. The chief priests seemed bent on a hush-hush policy; but *where is that body*? And where are those disciples who are supposed to have stolen the body? If they are still knocking about, why do *they* not step out and say frankly what happened? Why are they not rounded up and *made* to confess? Apparently they have become scattered. Yet nobody seems to know for certain.

And so the weeks have slipped away: but now, at length, the Day of Pentecost has dawned, on the first day of a new week, in accordance with the regulation of Leviticus xxiii. 16—on "the morrow after the seventh Sabbath" from the Passover. Once again Simon comes in through the city gates about nine o'clock in the morning, at the time of the morning sacrifice, and makes for the Temple.

As he nears the Temple, however, he finds the way blocked by a swelling concourse of curiously excited people. There is surprise and wonder and enquiry on every face. In the squash and jumble-up across the thoroughfare and the open area near the Temple, people are straining on tiptoe and craning their necks to see some person or persons who must surely be doing something extraordinary.

After his experience of a few Friday mornings ago, Simon is inclined to fight shy of this unorthodox-looking mix-up, only the signs and sounds this time indicate a much pleasanter sort of happening than that crucifixion episode. He edges cautiously in. Above the rapid murmur of mutual interrogation going on among the crowd, he now hears clear, ringing voices extolling Jehovah, first in what seems to be unadulterated Scriptural Hebrew, then in Aramaic, then in Greek. Yet the speakers are not priests or Levites or doctors of the law, or young men from the colleges. They are a group of youngish men whose dress at once shows that they are neither Pharisees nor Sadducees, neither fine-clad townsmen of Jerusalem nor curiosity-provoking foreigners. Simon is now right in among that ever-swelling collection of curious enquirers. He can see the speakers plainly. They rather give the impression of being fellows up from some of the smaller towns or villages, likely enough, as some are saying, from Galilee.

Simon gives a swift sweeping glance round that great throng. What a sight it is! What a sea of diverse garb and face! Is there any city in all the world which could exhibit such a cosmopolitan intermingling of men as Jerusalem during the Passover and Pentecost convocations? Here (in the words of Acts ii. 9–11) are "Parthians and Medes and Elamites, and dwellers in Mesopotamia and Judæa and Cappadocia, Pontus, Asia, Phrygia,

Pamphylia, Egypt, and *the parts of Libya about Cyrene*, strangers from Rome, Jews, proselytes, Cretes, Arabians." What a crowd!

But any wonder which Simon feels at the crowd is quickly and utterly eclipsed by his discovery, at this point, of the astounding phenomenon which has brought those hundreds of people together and holds them there nonplussed. There is something definitely supernatural here! Those ringing-voiced, plain-clad men certainly are expressing praise to God with a contagious exhilaration, but that alone would not account for the general astonishment. The fact is, they are expressing praise to God with a profundity and originality of thought and a supernatural felicity of eloquence which simply compel attention. They are declaring "the wonderful works of God," especially His wonderful works in redemption, in a way such as was never heard before. As though under sudden flashes of heavenly illumination, they quote and expound obscure passages of Holy writ and give startling new interpretations which arrest and amaze the hearers. What is more, the very faces and figures of this holy band rivet the eye. There is a simply seraphic look on their faces. Their whole personalities seem enrapt by the light of some tremendous discovery which has broken upon them.

Nor is that all. Every now and then, as though under some sudden superhuman impulse, different ones in that group stand out from the rest and deliver brief messages in some foreign tongue, which excites still keener astonishment in the minds of those foreigners in the multitude whose language is being spoken. In one language after another this group of plainly-clad preachers talk to the crowd, passing with artless ease from one language to another. Apparently each one of this group can speak in any language which he chooses!

What in the world can this thing mean?—that is the question which takes possession of the crowd. On the right hand and on the left, Simon hears men exclaiming, "Behold, are not all these which speak Galilæans? And how hear we every man in our own tongue wherein we were born?" (Acts ii. 7–8).

Of course, there are a few in this crowd, as in every other, who are ready with cheap and easy sarcasms; and from two or three quarters they call out, "These men are full of new wine!"

This seems to touch a very sensitive spot with that dozen or so men! They seem to take it as a bit of almost blasphemous irreverence. There is a pause. Then one who seems to be a leader among them stands forth alone to address the crowd. Oh, what a man! There may be nothing of the college tie about him; he is no don; yet there is a nobility and distinguishment all its own about that personality. He is a thoroughly manly man, evidently used to hard work and the open-air. And what character is written on that face! There is fire and dash and yet deep reflectiveness in those eyes, and in the expression there is a prepossessing blend of almost boyish frankness with mature seriousness. He lifts up his voice to the crowd. Oh, they all hear that voice. It is a voice according with the speaker's face—full, round, sonorous. And what beautiful diction! There is nothing academic about the phraseology: it is the vernacular; but the vocabulary and the choice of words and the finish of the sentences all evidence a keen mind and good taste. And there is a something more— there is a ringing tone of authority such as comes from a sense of certainty and intense earnestness. Everyone listens. There is a tense silence, the audience is gripped. What is it he is saying? —Simon of Cyrene listens to Simon Peter; and this is what he hears (though in Greek, not in English!)

"Ye men of Judæa, and all ye that dwell at Jerusalem, be this known unto you, and give ear unto my words. For these are not drunken, as ye suppose; seeing it is but the third hour of the day; but this is that which hath been spoken by the prophet Joel: *And it shall be in the last days, saith God, I will pour forth of my Spirit upon all flesh: and your sons and your daughters shall prophesy, and your young men shall see visions, and your old men shall dream dreams: yea and on my servants and on my handmaidens in those days will I pour forth of my Spirit; and they shall prophesy. And I will shew wonders in the heaven above, and signs on the earth beneath; blood, and fire, and vapour of smoke: the sun shall be turned into darkness and the moon into blood, before the day of the Lord come, that great and notable day: and it shall be, that whosoever shall call on the name of the Lord shall be saved.* Ye men of Israel, hear these words: Jesus of Nazareth, a man approved of God unto you by mighty works and wonders and signs, which God did by him in the midst of you, even as ye yourselves know; him, being delivered up by the determinate counsel and foreknowledge of God, ye by the hand of lawless men did crucify and slay: whom God raised up, having loosed the pangs of death: because it was not possible that he should be holden of it. For David saith concerning him:

> *I beheld the Lord always before my face;*
> *For he is on my right hand, that I should not be moved:*
> *Therefore my heart was glad, and my tongue rejoiced;*
> *Moreover my flesh also shall dwell in hope:*
> *Because thou wilt not leave my soul in Hades,*
> *Neither wilt thou give thy Holy One to see corruption.*
> *Thou madest known unto me the ways of life;*
> *Thou shalt make me full of gladness with thy countenance.*

Brethren, I may say unto you freely of this patriarch David, that he both died and was buried, and his tomb is with us unto this day. Being therefore a prophet, and knowing that God had sworn with an oath to him, that of the fruit of his loins he would set one upon his throne; he foreseeing this spake of the resurrection of the Christ, that neither was he left in Hades, nor did his flesh see corruption. This Jesus did God raise up, whereof we all are witnesses. Being therefore by the right hand of God exalted, and having received of the Father the promise of the Holy Ghost, he hath poured forth this, which ye see and hear. For David ascended not into the heavens: but he saith himself,

> *The Lord saith unto my Lord,*
> *Sit thou on my right hand,*
> *Till I make thine enemies the footstool of thy feet.*

Let all the house of Israel therefore know assuredly, that God hath made him both Lord and Christ, this Jesus whom ye crucified."

Yes, that is what they hear: and never did a preacher have a more concentrated hearing. There is an almost breathless stillness to hear him—scarcely a shuffle of the feet. Those hundreds of "devout men from every nation under heaven" fairly hang on the preacher's words. Their faces are a study—surprise, perturbation, alarm, but nowhere does there seem hostility. There is an ability and a courtesy and a convincing ring of certainty about that preacher which grip and sway his audience. And there is something more: there is an indefinable "atmosphere" generated through him which spreads like an invisible breath from God over that vast assembly. There is an abnormal influence operating in that crowd. There can be no mistaking it. They are breaking down under that resistless impact. Something is going to happen. They are at explosion point. And something *does* happen! They listen with bated breath as the preacher charges home the national guilt of crucifying God's long-promised miracle-attested Messiah for whom they and their fathers have been waiting for centuries—they listen until the preacher reaches the climactic words: "Therefore let all the house of Israel know assuredly that God hath made this same Jesus both Lord and Christ"—they listen to this point, and then some pent-up hearer calls out, with a sob in his voice, "Men and brethren, what shall we do?" and the cry is taken up and travels round again and again— "Men and brethren, what shall we do?" Hundreds of these men of Israel seem quite broken with grief. Many of them have seen and heard Jesus. They know well enough, as Pilate did, that the chief priests got Him put away through envy (Matt. xxvii. 18). They have seen some of the miracles which Jesus wrought. They have seen Lazarus whom He raised from the dead. They have heard some of the never-to-be-forgotten utterances which fell from His lips. They have heard the strange rumour about the disappearance of the body from the tomb. They have had their own thoughts despite the hush-hush policy of the Sanhedrim. And now here is the promised outpouring of the Spirit of Jehovah upon Israel. There is no doubt about it. Here are the signs— the unmistakable signs in these very men who are now speaking in "other tongues" as the Spirit gives them utterance! Jesus is the Messiah—the suffering Messiah of Psalm xxii. and Isaiah liii.

who is now risen and is "sharing the spoils" with the privileged of Israel. There is such a scene as Jerusalem has never witnessed before. Hundreds acknowledge Jesus as Messiah-Saviour. There are relays and relays of eager hearers. They all fall prey to that mighty message and that mysterious power. Hundreds more are converted, making a total (as Acts ii. 41 tells us) of some 3000 souls!

And Simon of Cyrene is among these first converts to the Lord Jesus. Yes, it surely is Simon whom we see here—none listening more intently than he. Somehow we cannot help thinking that Luke has Simon in mind, in this crowd, when he tells us (in Acts ii. 9-11) that the crowd is composed of "Parthians and Medes . . . and those *from the parts of Libya about CYRENE.*"

Watch Simon's face. Get into his thoughts. Oh, what memories flash back to the mind from that Friday morning seven weeks ago! What indescribable emotions stir within him! This wonderful Messiah, this crucified but now risen and ascended and glorified Jesus, who is both Lord and Christ, is that wonderful, wonderful man for whom he carried the cross that morning! Wonder of wonders! Oh, if only he had known at the time there would have been no reluctance! That supposed criminal was none other than the long-promised deliverer of Israel, whose name should be called "Wonderful, the mighty God, the Prince of peace, the everlasting Father"!

Simon listens spellbound. What he has thought to be the unhappiest indignity ever done to him has become the most transcendent honour that ever could be his. Of all the many hundreds who listen to Peter's Pentecostal sermon, none listens with just the rapt wonderment of Simon the Cyrenian. Amid the wholesome upheaval which follows Peter's preaching we lose sight of him in the enquiring crowd; but one thing is pretty certain—he is one of that first 3000 who hear and believe to the saving of their souls!

SCENE 3: A CROWNING WONDER

Simon is now back home again in Libya and in his own city of Cyrene. His long-planned, memorable visit to Jerusalem is over. All his brightest dreams in anticipation of it have been eclipsed by the actual transpirings of it. It dwarfs all other experiences of his life—and he is now well on in years (if we may surmise from certain dates which we are now about to mention). He can never forget it; and he can never be the same again, for he has found salvation, and has come back home a changed man.

What a story he has to tell! He can talk about it by the hour; and his wife and sons can *listen* by the hour, for never before did any returned pilgrim have such a story as he. How they listen—and shudder, as he tells them of that Friday morning when he was grabbed by the soldiers and forced to carry a criminal's gibbet to the execution mound outside the city! But how sympathetic they feel as he tries to describe the heart-melting look and tones and bearing of that prisoner! And oh, how their eyes grow round with wonder as he relates the simply staggering sequel! He tells how his interest was aroused in this Jesus of Nazareth. He tells of the words and behaviour of Jesus when on the cross, of the sudden blanket of darkness which covered the land, of the rending of the temple veil, and of other extraordinary accompaniments of that crucifixion. He tells about the widespread impression made by Jesus, and of the many authenticated miracles which he, Simon, had learned about since that Friday morning. He tells about the strange rumour regarding the disappearance of the corpse from the sepulchre, and about very many other things pertaining to those memorable weeks. And then, of course, he has his wife and sons almost open-mouthed as he describes that astounding climax on the day of Pentecost. He lives through it all again as he describes it. They can see how deeply his own feelings are stirred. Theirs are stirred too. He tells them of his conversion, how the strange power from heaven fell upon him, as it did upon hundreds more, how 3000 were converted on the same day, and another 5000 a few days later, and how, when he, Simon, left Judæa the whole country was alive with excitement concerning this crucified and resurrected Messiah Jesus, who had now ascended to heaven and poured out the Spirit promised by Jehovah through Joel and other prophets, and how the Gospel was to be preached to all peoples, and how Jesus would quickly return, in the power and glory of kingship, if Israel repented and accepted Him.

So Simon tells his story, and, as he does so, all unconsciously he falls into "preaching" the Gospel. He finds himself in deep concern about the conversion of his dear wife and family; and, in the mercy of God, they too become believers upon the Lord Jesus for the salvation of their souls!

How do we know all this? Well, it is just here that this and that and the other verse of Scripture lights up with guiding light to us. We turn back again to Mark xv. 21, and note again that Simon is there called "the father of *ALEXANDER AND RUFUS.*" This begins to have new significance when we reflect *when* and *where* and *why* Mark wrote his Gospel. He wrote it some 25 to 30 years after our Lord's ascension; and his reference to Alexander and Rufus simply by their names, without any need to explain who they were, indicates that they were well-known persons among those for whom Mark was primarily writing. This is no doubtful inference, for obviously it would have been pointless superfluity for Mark to explain Simon's identity by saying he was the father of two sons who themselves were unknown! The fact is, that Alexander, and Rufus were much more widely known than their father, and that is why Mark finds it needful to explain that Simon of Cyrene was the father of Alexander and Rufus.

There seem to be other reasons, too, why Mark thought well to add that Simon was the father of Alexander and Rufus. One of these is that Simon himself had died during this twenty-five or thirty years, and Mark's readers would not know that the man who helped to carry our Lord's cross was the deceased father of two outstanding Christian leaders among them. And another probable reason is that the family had now left Libya and gone to live in Rome.

Both these conjectures find augmented likelihood in another text which we are about to mention; but first recall *where* and *why* Mark wrote his Gospel. If early tradition is right (and there is much to be said for it) he wrote his Gospel *in Rome.* Mark himself was apparently a Roman citizen. His Hebrew name was "John," but his surname, "Markos," was Roman, and the

adding of such a surname was a usual badge of Roman citizen-
ship. This accords with the social standing of the family. The
description of his mother's house, in Acts xii., with its large room
and porch, and the mention of a Greek servant, suggests wealth;
and we know that Mark's uncle, Barnabas, was also a man of
means (Acts iv. 36). We know that after his conversion to the
Lord Jesus, Mark travelled widely, serving with Paul and Barnabas, then later with Barnabas alone (Acts xv. 36–39), and still
later with Paul again. We find him with Paul *in Rome* (Col. iv.
10, Philemon 24), and the last reference to him is a request of
Paul that Mark should *return* to him *at Rome* (2 Tim. iv. 11).

So Mark was a Roman citizen, and was often in Rome on
Christian service, and probably settled there for some time later.
And this at once accords with the distinctive characteristics of
his "Gospel." As Matthew was written primarily for Jews, and
Luke primarily for Greeks, and John primarily for Christians,
so Mark was written primarily for Romans. There are all sorts
of indications of this, into which we cannot go here: they are a
study in themselves. But at any rate the clear fact is that Mark's
Gospel, while not *exclusively* meant for any one class of reader,
was certainly meant *primarily* for Romans. There was real need
for such a writing, and that is why Mark wrote it.

Now it is to *these* readers that Mark speaks of Simon's sons,
Alexander and Rufus, as being so well-known. They were well-
known at Rome: and with this in mind turn now to that great
epistle which Paul wrote to Rome, and look up chapter xvi.,
where we have the longest and most interesting list of personal
greetings in all Paul's epistles. In verse 13 we read—

> "Salute *RUFUS*, chosen in the Lord, and
> *HIS MOTHER* and mine."

There can scarcely be doubt that this is the same Rufus. He
is a Rufus at *Rome*; he is evidently well-known among the
Christian brethren there, just as the Alexander and Rufus mentioned by *Mark* are well-known among the Romans for whom
he primarily writes; and there is no other New Testament Rufus.
What is more, it looks as though the great apostle Paul was at
one time a guest in the home of Rufus's mother, or that at any

rate she had in some tender way "mothered" him somehow and somewhere in his missionary travels, before she came to live in Rome; for he speaks of her as "his mother *and mine.*" She was Rufus's mother in the literal sense, and Paul's in a figurative sense. Two questions, of course, naturally suggest themselves: first, why is Simon himself not mentioned in Paul's greeting? and second, why is Rufus's brother, Alexander, not mentioned? In reply to the first, it is to be presumed, as we have already said, that in the intervening years Simon had died (which also may have mainly accounted for the removal of the home from Cyrene). In reply to the second, we may refer to the tradition, mentioned by Cornelius à Lapide, that his brother Alexander suffered early martyrdom as a Christian missionary, and was therefore already deceased at the time when Paul wrote his epistle to the Romans.

Paul's grateful and affectionate reference to Rufus's mother as "his mother *and mine*" may be because she had bestowed maternal care *again and again* upon the motherless apostle-missionary, and had thus endeared herself to him in a special way. And Paul's reference to Rufus is equally noteworthy—"Rufus, chosen in the Lord." Dr. Denny says that the Greek expression here has the sense of, *"that choice Christian."* He was one of the Lord's "specials," one of the élite in grace and gifts.

And now, with these data and reflections in mind see the sequel, the climax, the crowning wonder of Simon's cross-carrying ordeal on that Friday morning, the 11th April, A.D. 32. Simon discovers that all unknowingly he has carried the cross of the incarnate Son of God, and participated in the most tremendous event of all history. That which at first seemed the deepest of all humiliations becomes the highest of all honours. He himself becomes a saved man in Christ, and goes back as the first herald of the Gospel to Africa. His wife accepts the Gospel and becomes one with him in Christ. Both his sons accept the faith and become outstanding leaders among the early Christian community. One of them makes the supreme sacrifice for Christ as a missionary martyr; the other is widely known and beloved as "that choice servant of the Lord." Simon's wife becomes a sort of "second mother" to the great apostle Paul, and in her hospitable home he is refreshed and cared for. What a touching and lovely sequel to a trying and painful ordeal!

This, then is the drama of Simon of Cyrene. But we cannot turn our eyes away from the final scene without reflecting for a moment or two on one or two practical lessons which it brings home to us. The first of these is that very often out of our *acutest trials, ordeals, disappointments and humiliations come life's truest rewards and enrichments.* Away back in the Book of Judges (xiv. 14) we find Samson propounding a great riddle—

> "Out of the eater came forth meat,
> And out of the bitter came forth sweetness."

If I were asked for the truest answer to Samson's riddle in a *spiritual* sense, I would point to Simon of Cyrene, the man who helped carry the Cross. "Out of the bitter came forth sweetness." Out of the deepest shadow came the brightest discovery and joy.

That is the first and most obvious lesson; but as we recall these three "scenes" from Simon's story, we cannot but see that they constitute a threefold challenge to all Christian believers.

1. As Simon shared the bearing of the Cross in a literal sense, we must share it in a figurative sense. Let there be no shrinking. In many quarters to-day, the Cross is gilded over with sentimentalism. It costs nothing to bow and scrape before a crucifix, or to pay lip service to formal religion. But to say with Paul "God forbid that I should glory, save in the cross of our Lord Jesus Christ, by whom *the world is crucified unto me, and I unto the world*"—that still brings a stigma! Let us glory in it.

2. As Simon came into the wonderful blessing of Pentecost, so let it be our prayer that we ourselves may be filled by the Holy Spirit. Peter said: "The promise is unto you, and to your children, and to *all that are afar off,*"—and that included you and me!

3. As Simon went back home to evangelise his own kith and kin, and had the joy of bringing them to the Lord, so our own first concern should be the winning of our loved ones. Oh, to be His "living epistles" to other needy hearts around us!

THE MAN WHO REBUILT JERUSALEM

SCRIPTURE SNAPSHOT.

So I came to Jerusalem, and was there three days. And I arose in the night, I and some few men with me ; neither told I any man what my God put into my heart to do for Jerusalem ; neither was there any beast with me, save the beast that I rode upon. And I went out by night . . . and viewed the walls of Jerusalem, which were broken down, and the gates thereof were consumed with fire. . . .

Then said I unto them (the Jews and their leaders) : Ye see the evil case that we are in, how Jerusalem lieth waste, and the gates thereof are burned with fire. Come and let us build up the wall of Jerusalem, that we be no more a reproach. And I told them of the hand of my God which was good upon me, as also of the king's words that he had spoken unto me. And they said : Let us rise up and build. So they strengthened their hands for the good work.

But when Sanballat the Horonite, and Tobiah the servant, the Ammonite, and Geshem the Arabian, heard it, they laughed us to scorn, and despised us, and said : What is this thing that ye do ? Will ye rebel against the king ? Then answered I them, and said unto them : the God of heaven, he will prosper us, therefore we his servants will arise and build: but ye have no portion, nor right, nor memorial, in Jerusalem.

—Nehemiah ii. 11–20 (R.V.).

THE MAN WHO REBUILT JERUSALEM

"I am doing a great work . . . I cannot come down."
Nehemiah vi. 3.

IN THE spiritual lessons which it teaches, the little book of Nehemiah is a gem. It tells how, after wearying delays, the walls of Jerusalem were rebuilt by the repatriated Jewish "Remnant," under the virile leadership of Nehemiah, and how the people themselves were subsequently reinstructed in the Law which God had given to their nation long before, through Moses. This rebuilding of the city wall is a graphic object-lesson illustrating those truths which lie at the heart of all true service for God; and he who heeds the lessons here drawn in vivid lines will be a wise and successful builder in spiritual things.

In this book of Nehemiah, the man and the story are inseparably wedded to each other. How different a story the rebuilding of Jerusalem might have been if that huge burden and hazard had fallen to a man of different calibre from Nehemiah! If ever a crisis-hour was matched by a man, it was so in that city-rebuilding episode.

Yet it is not only the man who makes the story. It is almost equally true that the story makes the man. The perils and problems of the undertaking bring out all that is finest in the man. How often that happens! How much we owe to the difficulties and setbacks, the obstructions and oppositions, which have been permitted to try us! The things which we have thought were breaking us were in reality *making* us—as we now see in retrospect.

So then, let us follow this man from the beginning of his story to the time when the walls of Jerusalem were rebuilt. In the little book which bears his name we see Nehemiah in three capacities—(1) the cupbearer, (2) the wall-builder, (3) the governor. In this present study we are concerned with Nehemiah as the man who *rebuilt Jerusalem,* and we shall therefore limit ourselves to the first six chapters of the book, where we see Nehemiah first as the royal cupbearer (i. 1–ii. 10), and then as the wall-builder (ii. 11–vi. 19).

NEHEMIAH THE CUPBEARER (i. 1–ii. 10)

Nehemiah was "the son of Hachaliah" (i. 1), and apparently of the tribe of Judah (ii. 3). Evidently he was reared in exile, and in early manhood became attached to the Persian court, where he rose to the lucrative position of royal cupbearer before Artaxerxes Longimanus and queen Damaspia in the royal residence at Shusan. *"I was the king's cupbearer,"* he says of himself (i. 11). To us western and modern readers, that may sound a rather unimportant position, not unlike that of a butler among our aristocracy; but we are wrong in so thinking. To quote Dr. Angus, it was "an office which was one of the most honourable and confidential at the court"; and to quote Dr. W. M. Taylor, it was an office "referred to by ancient writers as one of great influence." We know the great influence which Pharaoh's butler had on behalf of Joseph; and we see what high rank the foul-tongued "Rab-shakeh" (or chief cupbearer) had in the empire of Assyria (2 Kings xviii.).

"The particular duties of the office proper," says Dr. Taylor, "were the washing of the royal cup, the tasting of its contents by pouring a few drops into the palm of the hand, and the presentation of it in a certain peculiar fashion to the king. But its special opportunity lay in the fact that the discharge of these duties gave access to the monarch in his freest and most familiar moments, and such was the value of the position that he who held it might aspire to the highest civil or military appointments without presumption, while if he did not choose to ask any favour for himself, he might, if he were at all unscrupulous, amass a fortune by selling his influence to others."

How did Nehemiah rise to this influential position? We believe that the answer to this question is supplied by what we see of his character in the succeeding chapters of the story—strict honesty, conscientious devotion to duty, unbending integrity in motive and purpose, and practical godliness. Sooner or later such character and principle always tell.

One day, while Nehemiah was in attendance at the royal court, his brother, Hanani, and a group of Jews, brought him such a pitiful report concerning the condition of Jerusalem and the restored Jewish community in Judæa that he was quite overcome with grief. He learned that his countrymen away in the homeland were in dire straits because, among other things, the city walls were still in ruins, and the gates remained just as they had been burned and broken by the Babylonians a hundred and forty years earlier. Walls and gates mean nothing to cities nowadays, but long ago, in the East, they meant almost everything. Those torn-down walls and gates left the inhabitants always open to attack and plunder by vicious neighbours; and it is quite probable that Hanani's report to Nehemiah was made the more poignant by the fact that the citizens of Jerusalem had at that very time been suffering in this way from the deceitful and treacherous peoples who surrounded them. Under such disadvantage and recurrent spoliation, discouragement had almost reached the point of despair.

Nehemiah, stricken with grief, thereupon gave himself to fasting and mourning and prayer (i. 2–11). During this process the conviction ripened in him that he himself should undertake the huge task of the rebuilding; but he was not his own master; and however difficult it might be to get *into* the Persian palace, when one *did* secure a position there it was even more difficult to get *out*. Nehemiah's grief and fasting, however, had so altered his appearance in four months that Artaxerxes asked what was wrong. The emperor's words seem to indicate that he had become really attached to his servant. None the less, as Dr. Kitto remarks, Nehemiah had reason enough to be *"very sore afraid"* (ii. 2), for it was considered a capital offence to appear sad in the royal presence (see also Esther iv. 2). Nehemiah answers with humble courtesy, not daring even now to make any request, but earnestly praying God to overrule; and the upshot is that Nehemiah is most generously commissioned to undertake the project which lies on his heart. Thus closes the first scene—Nehemiah the cupbearer. But let us now pick out two or three of the many lessons here. They may seem very simple, but they are very important.

First, *real godliness is not incompatible with earthly success.* Indeed it often happens that godliness is a first factor in promoting and furthering such success. One gets sick of hearing that to be a real Christian is impossible in the business world of to-day, and that to apply godly principles in modern commercial transactions is to invite bankruptcy. We could give many examples to the contrary. Certainly there is a price to pay, and there may be losses to incur; but observation convinces us that true Christian character and principle, allied to normal business ability, definitely contribute to success. If Nehemiah could keep his conscience unseared amid the cabals of that Persian court, so may we ourselves blend uprightness with success in modern business. Such present-day Nehemiahs are the salt of the commercial world. Better lose our job than sell our conscience! But in nine cases out of ten, keeping a good conscience will help us towards material as well as spiritual success, and will keep us steady when success actually comes.

Second, *we should use all influential position for God, as Nehemiah did.* Have we money?—we should use it as stewards, not as owners. Fundamentally we own nothing. Our money should be at our Lord's disposal, and should only be spent in ways which further the cause of Christ. Do we occupy high position?—our influence should be used in such a way as discreetly recommends Christ to those who come within the sphere of our influence. Have we outstanding gifts?—they should all be used to the glory of God. Every Christian, and especially those who hold influential office in the social structure, should live in the continual remembrance of Paul's words, "Ye are not your own; for ye are bought with a price; therefore glorify God in your body and in your spirit." God help us so to do!

Third, *we should ever be deeply concerned about the well-being of the Lord's people,* as Nehemiah was. What sorrow of heart, what earnest and persevering prayer there was when Nehemiah learned the state of things among Jehovah's people away in Judæa! Whenever there is to be a revival or some wonderful forward-movement of God's Spirit among men, some heart or hearts must become burdened as Nehemiah's did. Nehemiah was nothing less than principal cupbearer to a world-emperor, yet while his hand was on the jewelled chalice, his heart was set on the things of God. So was it with young William Carey, at the other end of the social scale, centuries later, who only repaired shoes that he might cobble his way to other continents with the redeeming message of the Gospel. Are our own hearts similarly stirred? Are we smug and comfortable in our own privileges, or are we really gripped with concern for the furtherance of the Gospel? Does it deeply trouble us that the churches to-day are so dead spiritually and so poorly attended, that true Gospel preaching is so rare, that godliness languishes both in high places and low, that multitudes of our fellow-Britishers are almost as ignorant of Gospel truth as the un-evangelised Kaffir in his kraal, that the unsparing scythe of death reaps a daily harvest of Christless millions for the grave and a dark beyond?

Does all this trouble us as it should? Oh, that our hearts might become burdened as Nehemiah's and William Carey's, for the rebuilding of Zion in the earth, for the reviving of the Church, and the salvation of the perishing! Oh, that we might feel the burden which was felt by that wonderful American soulwinner, the reclaimed drunkard, Sam Hadley, who, after visiting some of the New York night-clubs and beer haunts, on rescue work one night, was seen to lean wearily against a lamp-post and heard to groan, "Lord, the sin of this city is breaking my heart"! Do we wonder that God used such a man to save thousands? It is the Nehemiahs and William Careys and Sam Hadleys who become the real aristocracy of history, and whose names shine on as the stars for ever. God help us to learn, to feel deeply for souls, to pray with Nehemiah-like earnestness, and to follow the gleam from heaven! Nor must we give way to discouragement if answers to our prayers do not come by the next morning's post! Four months of fasting, praying, waiting, preceded the sudden providential turn which rewarded Nehemiah, for he commenced in the month Chisleu (December) and continued until the month Nisan (April)—and would have kept on still further if the answer had not come when it did. To quote Fenton's rendering of Ephesians vi. 18 we must persevere in our praying with "steady tenacity."

NEHEMIAH THE WALL-BUILDER (ii. 11–vi. 19)

Armed with royal authority, thrilled with a sense of Jehovah's overruling graciousness, and yet solemnised by keen appreciation of the hazards involved in his undertaking, Nehemiah sets off for Jerusalem, accompanied by an escort of Persian soldiers, and completes the journey in about three months. On his way he has to pass through the provinces of certain Persian satraps and governors. To those "beyond the river" (i.e., the Euphrates) he carries letters (ii. 7, 8) which he duly delivers (verse 9). Among such governors was a certain Sanballat, who, according to Josephus, was "satrap of Samaria." Also there was a certain "Tobiah the servant," who was either another petty governor or, more probably, a kind of secretary to Sanballat. These two, we are told, were greatly annoyed "that there was come a man to seek the welfare of the children of Israel" (verse 10). With these two, Nehemiah is now about to have much trouble. The two capitals, Jerusalem and Samaria were too near each other not to be rivals; and right from the time that Zerrubbabel had rejected the participation of the Samaritans in the rebuilding of the temple, ninety years before Nehemiah, an enmity had set in between the two people which survived even until Jerusalem was again destroyed by Titus in A.D. 70. The greater the prosperity of Jerusalem, the bitterer was the enmity of Samaria and the mongrel people who now inhabited it.

Nehemiah safely reaches Jerusalem, and, after an interval of three days, makes a secret survey of the ruins by night, so as to escape observation by hostile spies from Samaria. Nor does he divulge his mission even to the leaders at Jerusalem until he has made plans to ensure that the whole work shall be started and finished within a few weeks (ii. 12–18). His plan, so it turns out, was to *sectionise* the rebuilding among different work-parties all acting simultaneously, and each responsible for its own section of the wall (iii.). The plan so succeeded that in spite of opposition the wall was completely rebuilt in just over seven weeks

(vi. 15), after which solid folding-doors were placed at the gate-ways (vii. 1), guards were appointed, and regulations imposed concerning the closing of the gates at nightfall and their re-opening in the morning (vii. 3). Thus Nehemiah's main objective was achieved—all within six months of his mandate from Artaxerxes!

But what a six months of testing as well as of toil and triumph! These chapters should be read again and again, at regular intervals, by all Christian workers. They would save many a collapse of courage, many a heart-flutter of fear, many an eruption of impatience. Some of the most penetrating lessons of the book are found in this section on the rebuilding.

See here *the sleep-denying concern of the man who is burdened for the cause of God on earth*. See this man of prayer and faith going round those broken walls while darkness reigns over the scene and other men are asleep. It is a sight which stirs our spiritual sensibilities and provokes heart-searching thought. Whenever a true work of God is about to begin, some faithful, prayer-burdened servant of God has to take a journey like Nehemiah's —to weep in the night over the ruins, or to wrestle in some dark Gethsemane; and it is always such men as Nehemiah who become the inspirers and encouragers of others, undauntedly overcoming Satanic opposition and the idle jibes of worldly scoffers.

See here also *the blending of practical organising with intense spiritual-mindedness*. The task is sectionised and systematically prosecuted. Nehemiah was no believer in what the Plymouth Brethren sometimes call "a one-man ministry" (nor are we!). There must needs be leaders, but every one of the Lord's people without exception should have a part in the building up of the city of God on earth. It is interesting to notice that Nehemiah set each of the forty-two different work-groups to work on that part of the walls which was nearest to where its members themselves lived (iii. 10, 23, 29, 30). Their special job was in their own neighbourhood! This gave them a special interest in the work. Our first obligation for Christ is always our own neighbourhood. What happenings there would be to set the bells of heaven ringing if every true Christian believer were prayerfully to resolve —"I will make my own immediate locality my mission field. I will see to it that every family in it is regularly supplied with suitable evangelistic tracts. I will see to it that over a period of months every neighbour is earnestly and good-naturedly urged to come and hear such-and-such a minister who always gives a straight Gospel message. And I will pray for these neighbours every day, as long as I live in this neighbourhood"! Yes, what things might happen if all the Lord's people did that! It would certainly be one very telling way of blending the practical with the spiritual.

We find this blending of the practical with the spiritual all the way through the story of Nehemiah. In chapter iv. 9, for instance, we read: "We made our *prayer* unto God, and set a *watch* against them (the adversaries) day and night." Nehemiah never let presumption displace precaution. Again and again as we watch him we are reminded of Cromwell's famous words— "Trust in God, and keep your powder dry." We must never divorce the spiritual from the practical. In Christian work and war, agonising and organising should go together. In some senses, perhaps, organised Christianity is *over*-organised to-day, and we complicate our own progress by too elaborate machinery. Yet the real trouble is not so much the machinery itself as that the vital driving-force behind it all has largely failed. Organising has crowded out agonising. There is too much working before men and too little waiting before God. There is more and more motion, but less and less unction. More than ever before we wrestle with social problems in committees and conferences, but less than ever do we wrestle on our knees against evil spirit-powers which lie behind the social evils of our day. Our denominations are becoming more and more like elaborately dressed-up corpses! Nearly everybody in committee has a fine programme, but scarcely anybody seems to have a real spiritual burden! The practical has overridden the spiritual, and when that happens the practical becomes utterly *un*practical. It is the Nehemiahs whom God uses—who *blend* the practical and the spiritual.

HAZARDS OF THE WALL-BUILDING

But perhaps the most telling lessons of all in this story of Nehemiah occur in connection with the *obstructions and setbacks* which Nehemiah had to overcome in those months of rebuilding. There were three forms of opposition from *without*—scorn (iv. 1–6), force (iv. 7–23), craft (vi. 1–19). And there were three forms of hindrance from *within*—debris (iv. 10), fear (iv. 11–14), greed (v. 1–13). Each is a lesson, a study in itself, strikingly paralleling with what we are up against to-day in a spiritual sense.

OPPOSITION FROM WITHOUT

Scorn (iv. 1–6).

Take the opposition which Nehemiah encountered from outside. First it took the form of *scorn*. In chapter iv. 1–3, we read:

"But it came to pass that when Sanballat heard that we builded the wall, he was wroth, and took great indignation, and mocked the Jews. And he spake before his brethren and the army of Samaria, and said, What do these feeble Jews? Will they fortify themselves? Will they sacrifice? Will they make an end in a day? Will they revive the stones out of the heaps of the rubbish which are burned? Now Tobiah the Ammonite was by him, and he said, Even that which they build, if a fox go up he shall even break down their stone wall."

Never was there more derisive sarcasm than in Sanballat's question: "What do these feeble Jews?" And that is exactly the first reaction of the worldly-wise to-day towards the spiritually-minded minority scattered through the churches. "What do these feeble folk?" they ask contemptuously. What are a few little prayer meetings compared with a U.N.O. or Unesco, or a revolutionary change-over to a Socialist Government or a United Conference of Nations? What is this paltry idea about converting people one by one compared with scientific, legislative, educational, economic and sociological programmes which can affect millions at a sweep?

That is always how the world talks. It judges things by their outward dimensions. It hails the imposing schemes of political and other leaders, but affects scorn for the seemingly feeble spiritual methods of the Lord's "little flock." To all younger Christian men and women I would say: Do not be surprised by

the world's scorn at the spiritually-minded minority among pro-
fessing Christians. Speaking roundly, the Lord's people are not
the brilliant or affluent section of society. "Not many wise men
after the flesh, not many mighty, not many noble, are called"
(1 Cor. i. 26). Do not be surprised, therefore, if you are scorned
for your attachment to the Lord's people. And do not be *deceived*
by it either. Remember, the world's scorn is the scorn which
springs from spiritual blindness. Again and again events have
turned such scorn back upon the scorners, and they have been
humiliated as Sanballat and Tobiah were when godly Nehemiah
completed the rebuilding of the wall. The mightiest movements
for human uplift have originated with Christian prayer-groups,
as witness the Methodist revival, which saved England from
revolution, and ushered in an era of progress which lifted her to
leadership among the nations. Yet even the mightiest spiritual
movements, at least in their beginnings, have encountered the
world's scorn—either real or pretended; and we ourselves must
be ready for it.

It is instructive to notice the *circumstances* which were supposed to justify the scorn of Sanballat and Tobiah towards Nehemiah and his undertaking. First, there was the supposed impossibility of the undertaking—"Will they revive the stones?"
Second, there was the feebleness of the personnel—"these feeble
Jews." Third, there was the seeming unlikeliness of any Divine
intervention to help them—"Will they sacrifice? Will they make
an end in a day?" (i.e., Do they think that the God to whom
they sacrifice will miraculously cause them to finish the otherwise impossible task in one day?) Could anything be more
modern than that? Those are just the three main grounds on
which the world still scorns Gospel effort. First, there is the supposed impossibility of the undertaking. When we say that religious
revival is the greatest need of the hour, we get the scornful
rejoinder, "What! do you think you can bring about by that
means what all the wisest brains in high places cannot bring
about?" Second, there is the feebleness of the personnel. When
we say that the Gospel is the only real hope for men and nations,
the world sneers, "See what a feeble folk these Gospelisers are,
in number, status, wealth, culture, mental capacity!" Third,

there is the seeming unlikeliness of any Divine intervention. When we say that the first need is prayer, the world just laughs at us and asks, "Do you think the Almighty will take any notice? Do you think you can bring God round just to *your* way of thinking? If God takes any active interest at all in human affairs, why does He not do something to get humanity out of its present mess, without prayer meetings having to be held all the time?"

But now look at the *real reasons* for the scorn of Sanballat and Tobiah. First, there was hatred and anger against Jehovah and His people—"He (Sanballat) was *wroth*." His scorn was simply a covering for this. Second, there was ignorance and unbelief. Sanballat and Tobiah did not know the true God and His purposes through the covenant people. Third, Sanballat's scorn was simply a trick to hide the fact that he had no genuine ground at all for opposing Nehemiah. Even so is it to-day. The first real reason why the world opposes us is that Satan is behind it, and because the natural man hates that Gospel which must expose his sin before it can save his soul. The second real reason for the world's scorn is ignorance and unbelief—and very often when the ignorance is removed the unbelief is removed too. The third real reason for the world's scorn is *its inability to find any genuine argument against the Gospel.*

Well, how did Nehemiah meet the scorn of Sanballat and Tobiah? Verses 4, 5 and 6 in that same fourth chapter tell us. He just kept on praying and kept on building. "Hear, O our God," he says; "for we are despised." And after his prayer he adds, "So built we the wall . . . for the people had a mind to work." That is the way to meet scorn—not by counter-scorn! The scorn of Sanballat and Tobiah soon began to look stupid as the walls of Jerusalem rose higher and higher. Always our best answer to the world's scorn is to keep on praying to God for Pentecostal blessing, and keep on striving to win souls for Christ. God always honours such earnest prayer and effort. It is always a big victory for the devil if he can laugh us out of some worthy work for Christ, and I fear he manages this far too often. We do well to learn a lesson from Nehemiah! Most of us need to be more sensitive to the approbation of God, and less sensitive to the ridicule of men.

Force (iv. 7–23).

But look again at this opposition which Nehemiah encountered from outside. When taunts and sneers failed it took a more menacing form. Scorn gave place to *force*. Taunts became threats, and sneers became plots. Such enemies as Sanballat and Tobiah were not the sort to be content with venting their spleen in idle mockery. Their keenest shafts of sarcasm were lost on a devout soul like Nehemiah. So scorn now gives place to force. Read again in that fourth chapter, from verse 7 onwards.

> "But it came to pass that when Sanballat and Tobiah and the Arabians and the Ammonites and the Ashdodites heard that the walls of Jerusalem were made up and that the breaches began to be stopped, then they were very wroth, and conspired, all of them together, to come and fight against Jerusalem, and to hinder it. Nevertheless, we made our prayer unto our God, and set a watch against them day and night, because of them."

Things certainly looked pretty serious. The opposition had now developed into a formidable alliance—Sanballat, Tobiah, Arabians, Ammonites, Ashdodites! It is remarkable (or is it?) how again and again mutual enemies will become mutual friends to make common cause against the people of God. Pilate and Herod patched up their quarrel and became "friends" in their joint condemnation and abuse of Jesus (Luke xxiii. 12). Romanism and Paganism have joined hands before to-day against the true Protestant faith. Communist Russia and Nazi Germany have shaken hands in common purpose against Christianity. And we shall see more of this kind of thing as the present age draws to its end. We must never be surprised at it.

Look at the characteristics of this new opposition against Nehemiah. It was *combined*—"they conspired, all of them." It was *rabid*—"they were very wroth" (verse 7). It was *wily*—"Our adversaries said: They shall not know" (verse 11). It was *ruthless*—"to slay . . . and cause the work to cease" (verse 11). History has repeated itself again and again in this respect since Nehemiah's day, and doubtless will do so again before Christ

returns and Satan is interned in the abyss; for behind all such
deadly antagonisms to the work of God is Satan himself.

And what was it that aroused this armed hostility? Had
Nehemiah been scheming against these people? Had Nehemiah
sent armed bands to prey upon them? No, it was simply that
the walls of Jerusalem were going up (verse 7). It is ever so. The
most innocent and inoffensive work or witness for God will often
occasion the most cruel opposition of the world, the flesh and the
devil. Our Lord Jesus had no need to denounce the false leaders
of His day in order to incite attempts by them upon His life. His
holy character, apart from anything else, was such a standing
condemnation of their hypocrisy that it was enough in itself to
ignite their hateful pride into murderous flame. We see the same
thing in the martyrdom of Stephen. Bunyan's *Pilgrim's Progress*
tells us that the innocent devoutness of Christian and Faithful at
Vanity Fair was enough by itself to provide occasion for deadly
mischief against them. The very fact that a work is for God will
arouse the ruthless opposition of Satan-controlled men. The very
fact that a life is lived for God is enough to stir the hate of men
whose sinful ways are exposed by the contrast.

We must not be surprised even to-day if the Lord's enemies
resort to force. And if this happens what are we to do? Well, what
did Nehemiah and his company do? They did as before—kept on
praying and kept on working; only now they had to join *watching*
with praying, and *warring* with working. See verses 9 and 17.

"We made our prayer unto God, and set a watch against them,
day and night" (verse 9).

"Every one with one of his hands wrought in the work, and
with the other hand held a weapon" (verse 17).

Was not prayer alone enough, then? Why this setting of a
watch and this arming with weapons if they trusted the Lord?
It was because Nehemiah was not the fanatic to blunder into the
delusion that faith is presumption. There are situations in which
we can do absolutely nothing for ourselves, and then it is perfectly
right to trust God to do absolutely everything; but in other cases,
where there are reasonable precautions which we ourselves can
take, we ought to take them, and it is presumption *not* to take

them, unless God clearly reveals that we are not to do so. Beware of letting a flighty zeal put an emotional presumption in the place of sensible precaution! Many have suffered through this, and then have unfairly blamed God. Prayer is never to be an excuse for carelessness. We must not confuse *trusting* God with *tempting* Him. Petition without precaution is presumption.

Praying, watching, working, warring! How all this speaks to us to-day! We are not suggesting for a moment that when physical force is used against Christians they should resort to physical weapons, as Nehemiah was obliged to do; but there is a spiritual application. There is a proper place for resisting and attacking and exposing error, deception, falsehood, and sin, on the part of those who oppose the truth as it is in Christ Jesus. Nor must we shrink from such warring, whatever the risk or cost. It is with good Scriptural reason that we sing:

> Stand up, stand up for Jesus,
> Ye soldiers of the Cross!

There is a place for controversy. Paul's epistles show us that. There is a place for fighting error, and demolishing Satan's citadels in the mental and social life of our fellow-creatures; but warring must never exclude *building*. The negative must not crowd out the positive. As it was with Nehemiah's band, we must have a sword in one hand and a trowel in the other. We must build as well as battle. The walls must go up, for in the long run the best warring and defence is to build up the walls of truth! They used force against John Bunyan; they flung him into Bedford prison; but the building of the wall went on, for it was in that prison that the immortal *Pilgrim's Progress* came into being. Five times they put John Wesley into Dorset jail; but the building of the wall went on, and the Methodist revival spread further and further. May the Lord show us how to blend praying and watching and working and warring and building and battling—in the Holy Spirit! We must keep at it to-day, against all the attacks of the enemy—praying unceasingly, watching against encroachments of sin in our lives, wielding the sword of Scriptural truth against error and sin, and building up the walls of God's spiritual Zion by daily witnessing for Christ.

Craft (vi. 1–19).

But there was yet another kind of opposition from exterior foes which Nehemiah had to encounter. When scorn and force had failed, Sanballat and Tobiah and their confederates resorted to *craft*. This is always the order adopted by the arch-enemy of souls against ourselves. What he cannot do by scorn and force he would do by guile and cunning; and he is always more dangerous as an "angel of light" than as a "roaring lion."

The craft of Nehemiah's enemies took four turns. First they tried *pretence* (vi. 1–4.) "Come, let us meet together in one of the villages in the plain of Ono." This was an enticement to a pretendedly friendly conference on neutral ground, presumably with the suggestion that an alliance should now be made between Nehemiah and themselves. But Nehemiah saw through their hypocrisy (verse 2), and each time they repeated their request he repeated his reply: "I am doing a great work; I cannot come down" (verse 3). This is ever the one safe answer to such pretence—uncompromising separation, whatever the threatened consequences.

Next they tried *bluff* (verses 5–9). They said that a charge was being lodged with the emperor against Nehemiah and the Jews, to the effect that they were planning rebellion, and that Nehemiah's only answer to this was to "take counsel with themselves." Nehemiah's reply is frank denial, renewed prayer, and a continued separation.

Next, and worst of all, they managed to intrigue some of Nehemiah's own kinsmen, and thus employed *treachery* against him (verses 10–14). It was realized that Nehemiah's inspiring influence rested mainly on his grand moral character, and the scheme, therefore, was to get him so to act, on the advice of seeming friends, that his conduct would look suspicious, and provide ground for an evil report. Even among the prophets in Jerusalem there were some who allowed themselves to be bribed to bring this about. Nehemiah, however, refused to do the cowardly or shady thing even on the advice of a prophet. The perfidy of these Judases among his own followers was a cutting sorrow to Nehemiah, but he overcame by his courageous honesty and by prayer (verses 11, 14).

It seems an awful thing to say, yet it is true, that there are
betrayers like Shemaiah and Noadiah (verses 10–14) in most
Christian congregations to-day—men and women who have professed conversion to Christ, who share in the fellowship and
labours of the saints, who nevertheless seem to find a strange,
cruel pleasure in the fall of a Christian leader. To his face they
are friendly, fussy, saintly, but behind his back they are mischief-
makers. They profess loyalty and concern, yet if he slips or falls
they love to gossip it among the brethren or talk it round the
town. Oh, what heart-pangs such disloyal brethren give to Christian ministers, pastors, superintendents, and leaders! They are
Tobiah's Quislings, Satan's fifth-columnists. They call Christ,
"Lord, Lord," but they will find their place at last with other
liars in the fire that is never quenched! All that the Christian
leader can do in his dealing with them is just to keep on building
for God through "evil report and good report" (2 Cor. vi. 8),
courageously refusing all shady expedients, keeping a clean conscience, and continually casting himself on God by prayer.

But there is something still further to be added. Nehemiah's
enemies did not cease their crafty activities even when this special
bit of treachery had failed. They sought continually to unnerve
and discourage Nehemiah through *cliques of compromised
brethren* (verses 17–19).

> "Moreover, in those days the nobles of Judah sent many letters
> unto Tobiah, and the letters of Tobiah came unto them. For
> there were many in Jerusalem sworn unto him because he
> was the son-in-law of Shechaniah the son of Arah; and his
> son Johanan had taken the daughter of Meshullam the son
> of Berechiah. Also they reported his good deeds before me,
> and uttered my words to him. And Tobiah sent letters to
> put me in fear."

It must have been a sore problem to Nehemiah, to find that
many of the leading men in Judah were hobnobbing by post with
Tobiah, and that many, indeed, were "sworn unto him" because
both he and his son had married into Israel. The artful Tobiah
had become a son-in-law to a leader in Israel with a large following; then his son had taken a Jewish girl to wife; so that Tobiah

was now both a son-in-law and an uncle to Israelite people; and there had grown up a clique in Jerusalem who let social and family ties with Tobiah override moral and spiritual duty. Oh, how compromise complicates things! These leaders in Israel should never have allowed such inter-marriage, but they were weak, they compromised, and now the godly man must pay a penalty of suffering. Nehemiah would never feel sure of this man and that man and the other man because of this matrimonial compromise and divided loyalty.

And does not the same sort of thing curse Christian congregations to-day? How often it ties the hands and paralyses the lips and breaks the hearts of earnest Gospel ministers! Here is a minister who would hit out against drinking and smoking, but he finds that his office-bearers have compromised on those two things, and to speak his full mind on the subject would mean so antagonising them as to occasion the end of his ministry among them. Here is a servant of God who feels that he ought to denounce the evil influence of the modern cinema industry, but among his leaders and congregation there are those who frequent the picture house, and if he were to speak out on this as he feels he ought, he would soon find the removal van at the manse door. A faithful pastor feels duty-bound to warn his brethren against clandestine societies such as the Masons, but some of his members who are most influential socially, though not spiritually, are Masons, and they would soon see to it that the voice of the Lord's prophet was turned to a different locality rather than have their consciences probed on the matter. Sometimes there are office-bearers or members who justly merit rebuke, but the pastor finds that if he opposed this man or that man he would at once alienate a whole clique who are so one with the trouble-maker that they would support him whether he were right or wrong, and would not hesitate to make the pastor's life among them almost unendurable. Out-and-out Christian leadership and ministry is not an easy thing in these days. Many a man in the ministry gives way, bit by bit, for reasonable comfort's sake; but he ceases to be a real Nehemiah. It is not easy to maintain the Nehemiah position; yet in the end it is the only one which wears the crown of Divine approbation and true success.

HINDRANCES FROM WITHIN

We have seen something of the opposition which came to
Nehemiah from outside Jerusalem, but now look at the hindrances
which he encountered from the *inside*. They were threefold—
debris (iv. 10), fear (iv. 11–14), greed (v. 1–13).

Debris (iv. 10).

First, there was the problem of *debris*. "And Judah said: The
strength of the bearers of burdens is decayed, and there is much
rubbish, so that we are not able to build the wall." We can easily
understand such discouragement. At the very beginning of the
rebuilding Sanballat had sarcastically referred to the huge "heaps
of the rubbish." It must have seemed a heart-breaking as well
as a back-breaking job to get without all this before each part
of the wall could be reconstructed; and now there had needed to
be a reduction of workmen, owing to the appointing of a guard
against attack from outside (verse 9), so that the remaining
labourers removing the rubbish seemed near to exhaustion.

This has a pathetic counterpart in much Christian work to-day.
There is many a devout servant of the Lord who cannot get on
with the wall God has given him to build, because of the hindrance
through "much rubbish." Oh, the "rubbish" in many of our
churches to-day! I recently received a letter from a minister in
the south of England asking advice whether to leave or stay on
at a certain church. It is impossible, he says, to make any spiritual
headway because of "much rubbish." The preceding ministers
were Modernists. They have deposited all sorts of doubts and dis-
beliefs in the people's minds about the Bible, so that now his own
references to the Scriptures are largely discredited and his messages
thwarted. He cannot get on with a constructive work because of
this Modernist rubbish-deposit which needs clearing away first!

Some days ago I interviewed a gentleman and his wife who
have felt forced to leave a church in Scotland for a similar reason.
They are a fine couple—he a city businessman, she a gifted
teacher, and just about as unquarrelsome a couple as one could
wish to meet; but they can stick this church no longer. They

have done their best to keep an evangelical work going; but the minister does not believe in the virgin birth of Christ, or in the bodily resurrection of Christ, or in the promised second advent of Christ, or in the Cross as a substitution and atonement, or in the inspiration of the Bible except in a very loose way. With such "rubbish" from the pulpit, any real building for Christ in *that* church is impossible.

But that is not the only sort of "rubbish." In a letter from another minister in England I read: "The people here have no ear for any spiritual challenge. They resent it. For years the place has been run on whist drives, social evenings including dancing, and so on. In trying to get hold of the young men and women demobilised from war service I wanted something vital and worthwhile, but the deacons voted solidly against it and insisted on a 'Games Evening.' The minister before me made himself popular by these things, and they think me narrow. They have no financial worries because a well-to-do member gives liberally. The church is really more like a club. I thought it might be a step in the right direction if we started a C.E., but it has found no response. What am I to do? All these other things block the way, and there is no appetite for saving truth."

Yes, indeed, "there is much rubbish, so that we are not able to build the wall"! And beyond any doubt, such discouragement from *within* is far more heart-breaking than opposition from without.

Fear (iv. 11–14).

But there was another discouragement from within, namely, *fear*. Jews from outlying districts brought repeated warning that a surprise attack was being planned by Nehemiah's enemies (verses 11, 12). This spread fear among the workers. Even the "nobles" and "rulers" among them, who should have rallied the people, showed the same symptom (verse 14). Once again Nehemiah seems alone; and what a hero he is as he stands there in solitary courage, seeking to turn fear to faith among the rest! "Be ye not afraid of them: remember the Lord, great and terrible, and fight for your brethren, your sons and your daughters, your wives and your houses" (verse 14).

"Be not afraid!" Nothing is more paralysing than fear; and how often it paralyses evangelical work to-day! It arises mainly from looking at circumstances and consequences instead of looking to God. Nehemiah's men were scared by the numerical superiority of Sanballat's forces. There is a parallel to-day. Never did the foes of evangelical Christianity seem bigger and deadlier than now. In Soviet Russia and Hitlerite Germany we have seen the State itself solidly against it—with Siberian exile or Nazi concentration camps as the penalty for faithfulness to Christ. Is it surprising that fear should have blanched many a cheek and stifled many a testimony?

Even here in Britain, how fear paralyses evangelical effort! How many Protestant leaders are afflicted with strange dumbness through secret fear of the Roman Catholic church! How many ministers there are who shrink from out-and-out identification with the evangelical cause in its fight against Modernism, against Sunday secularisation, and against other God-dishonouring movements of the present hour because the odds against us seem overwhelming, and because the consequences in loss of friends or prestige or income would be hard to endure! And how many there are among the rank and file in our churches who are kept dumb through fear! They are afraid that the teachings of the evangelical Christian faith can no longer hold their own against the popular ideas of life which modern science and psychology have spread abroad. Is there anything which destroys initiative more than fear? Does there seem to be a fatal lack of initiative on the part of the evangelical forces in our land to-day? Is it due to fear?

It is instructive to see how Nehemiah turned the tables on this fear which had beset his men. First, they were to *look to God* instead of at circumstances. "Remember the Lord, great and terrible!" cries Nehemiah (verse 14). They were to remember that they were truly in the will of God, that they were truly fighting for the cause of God, and that God was therefore really with them. They were to remember that their God was the "great and terrible," in alliance with whom final defeat was impossible. Yes, that was the first thing—"Remember the Lord!" It was a grand battle-cry to give them.

Second, they were to *reflect* on the issues. "Fight for your brethren, your sons and your daughters, your wives and your houses" (verse 14). Everything was at stake! No mercy could be expected from their spiteful foe.

Third, they were to be *armed in readiness* (verses 16–23). Henceforth they were to hold a tool in one hand and a weapon in the other. What wisdom there was in this union of sword and trowel! Even the nuisance diversion of anti-invasion preparation must not stop the building of the wall, for in the long run that rebuilt wall would itself be the supreme defence. Even battling must not exclude building!

How these three things come home to ourselves to-day! We must *"remember the Lord."* Somehow we have got our eyes away from God, so we are afraid of men. Most of the churches seem to be looking to human contrivance instead of to the Divine power. Is that an overstatement? Then what about the decline or complete disappearance of the prayer meeting in many places? God has become unreal. Therefore fear takes the place of faith. There is no antidote to fear like a vivid God-consciousness. "Remember the Lord!" cries Nehemiah. "Remember Jesus Christ . . . risen!" exclaims Paul. "Lo, I am with you always" says our living Lord. Oh, that we might really fix our eyes and our hearts upon Him!

And, second, we must *keep the issues ever in mind.* Oh, there is a lot of vague thinking and hazy seeing and spineless toleration to-day in the name of Christian liberty. I am no lover of the drastic. I prefer the smoother course of procedure any day; but I am sure it is time that many of us honestly faced up to the clear-cut difference between true, evangelical Christianity on the one hand, and the Modernist and Romanist and Secularist camps on the other. If the distinctive doctrines of the evangelical faith are really true concerning the Bible and the person of Christ and the shed blood of Calvary and the message of the Gospel, then the distinctive doctrines of the Modernists and the Romanists are wrong. And the issues are immeasurably graver than were those in the Nehemiah episode. Souls are at stake! Eternal destinies hang in the balance! The well-being of whole nations is involved! Yes, if we ponder the magnitude and momentousness of the issues in our struggle, surely courage must flame up in our hearts again, as it did in the days of the Protestant reformers.

And third, we must not forget our need of being *armed to fight*. Our weapons are: (1) the Bible, which is "the sword of the Spirit"; (2) prayer, which can avail to thwart error just as much as to save souls; (3) the continually-renewed infilling of the Holy Spirit. The possession of such weapons should destroy fear. In the power of this threefold provision, our preaching, teaching, writing, and individual witness-bearing can break Satanic opposition at every point. Yet even warring against enemies must not absorb energy which should go to wall-building. The destructive must not displace the constructive. Building must go along with battling; for in the end the best way to pull down error is to propagate truth. We most win the war when we best build the wall!

Greed (v. 1–13).

Alas, there was a third hindrance from within, and it was even worse than the other two. It was a plague of *greed*. This came nearer to wrecking Nehemiah's project than all the stratagems of Sanballat and Tobiah, for it threatened internecine strife among Nehemiah's own men. The circumstances were most disturbing. Many of the people, in order to raise money with which to buy corn (verse 3) or to pay tribute (verse 4) had been obliged to mortgage land holdings, and in some cases even to pledge their sons and daughters; and the richer Jews, instead of sinking private interests in the critical public need, had selfishly exploited it until a point was reached where there was an outcry. There seem to have been five factors responsible for the food crisis. First there was over-population (verse 2) due to influx of immigrants and the smallness of the areas they were allowed to occupy; second, a recent famine (verse 3) due probably to the unsettled state of the country, which must have seriously impeded agricultural and pastoral occupations; third, the heavy taxation to meet the Persian tribute (verse 4); fourth, the difficulty of importing corn because of roving enemies; and fifth, the heavy taxing by former governors (verse 15).

Some of these factors had brought the bread crisis on gradually, but probably the rebuilding of the wall and the defence of the

city had hastened it to the point of acuteness by temporarily
preventing artisans and tradesmen from plying their usual occupations. Some of the people must have been on the brink of
starvation and penury to have let their children go into slavery
with no prospect of redeeming them (verse 5). First they had
needed to sell property for money to buy bread; then, as the price
of bread had risen because of its scarcity, they had spent their
money for food; and now they had neither food nor money. The
wealthier Jews, who could have averted such a situation, had
taken a monstrously cruel advantage, acquiring the lands and the
money and even the sons and daughters of their poorer countrymen! I suppose one might unearth black-marketing and racketeer-
ing in almost any crisis; but the most pathetic thing of all is when
a work of *God* is disfigured by such base opportunism.

If Satan cannot ruin a work for Christ to-day by "much
rubbish" or by "fear" of one sort or another, he will try to do
so through self-seeking and other wrong motives between Christian and Christian. He will seize on every possible circumstance
to provoke this; and his heart-rending success is known in earth
and heaven! How disheartened Nehemiah must have been!
And how disheartened many a godly minister is to-day when he
finds that even among his keenest and ablest workers there are
wrong motives and feelings which thwart blessing and frustrate
revival despite all the praying and working to that end! This
one has been wronged by that one, and cannot forgive it. That
one has a grudge against another one, and will not forego it.
Another one was misjudged by still another, and cannot forget
it; and so on. They are one in conviction but not in affection.
They are united against the foe without, but they are divided
among themselves within. And, although it may seem almost
unbelievable, there are those who can maintain a peculiar outward zest for Christian work and church activities yet at the
same time take mean advantage of their trustful comrades for
the sake of personal gain! Oh, there are strange anomalies and
enigmas! Human nature is for ever springing surprises.

See now how Nehemiah dealt with this trouble. First, he challenged the offenders by prompt, even drastic, action (verse 7).
Second, he appealed to them by his own example (verses 8–11).

Third, the offending party admitted their blame and made restitution (verses 12, 13). Oh, what a good thing is promptness, frankness, boldness, in such matters!

So many of us who have leadership are afraid of what the consequences might be for ourselves if we forced this or that wrong relationship among our people into the light and got it squarely dealt with. Yet how the harm multiplies when such things are allowed to drag on! As already said, we are not fond of drastic measures; but do not most of us err to the opposite extreme? We say that we do not like to "meddle" or "interfere" or "offend." It is easy to mistake cowardice for discretion.

The trouble in Nehemiah's day was put right because the offenders, being frankly charged with wrong, admitted their blame, and put the wrong right.

Thus the setback through greed, like the other troubles, was overcome, and the building of the wall went on. Look back, once more, over the difficulties which brave Nehemiah encountered and surmounted—from *without,* scorn (iv. 1–6), force (iv. 7–23), craft (vi. 1–19); from *within,* debris (iv. 10), fear (iv. 11–14), greed (v. 1–13). In each case the difficulty becomes more acute and deadly, but in each case the victory becomes more telling, until, stone by stone, and day by day, despite all opposition from without and all hindrance from within, *the wall is completed!*

These, then, are some of the lessons which come home to us from Nehemiah's rebuilding of that city wall. May we read, mark, learn, and act accordingly! The days in which we live have an intensity and complexity such as eclipses that of all former times. The need is vast. The issues are tremendous. The time is short. The wall must be built, even "in troublous times." God help us to keep at it—warring and working, watching and waiting, battling and building! Let us mark this man, Nehemiah, the man who rebuilt Jerusalem, and keep him in mind as we work for God to-day under difficult conditions. He will be an inspiration to us. God is building with us; and at last we too shall certainly see the walls of God's "New Jerusalem" completely built up, and "the nations shall walk in the light of it."